M000034206

Trust, Inc.

A Practical Guide to the Alignment of Values, Organizational Goals and Results

by Judith Rogala, M.B.A.
and Carol Orsborn, Ph.D.

AMP&RSAND, INC.
Chicago, Illinois

ABOUT THE COVER

The level is a great tool and metaphor for this book. It tells you, without equivocation, if things are in balance. To perfect the alignment of an object you have to shift it until the bubble sits precisely between the centerlines. The same could be said of one's personal and professional life. If your values and goals are not aligned, results will be off. We hope that this practical guide will serve you well.

Copyright © 2005 by Judith Rogala and Carol Orsborn

All rights reserved. No part of this book may be reproduced in any form or by any electronic or mechanical means, including information storage and retrieval systems, without permission in writing from the publisher, except by a reviewer who may quote brief passages in a review.

First Edition

ISBN 0-9761235-0-9

Design: David Robson, Robson Design

Published by Ampersand, Inc. Chicago, Illinois

Printed in the United States of America

DEDICATION

*To all those in organizational life who have
the willingness to trust, the wisdom to question
and the courage to lead.*

CONTENTS

"Trust: Belief in honesty and reliability of another; confident expectations, hope."

Webster's *New World Dictionary*

The Alignment of Trust and Ethics

Is it possible to build rather than breach trust while going about the day-to-day business of leading our divisions and companies?

This question may seem foolhardy at first, given that rarely does an entire day go by without some individual or company making headline news in regard to a wide range of embarrassing or destructive ethical lapses. And yet, at the same time, there are individuals and organizations that somehow find a way to rise above the temptations and pitfalls to become internationally respected and rewarded for their values. What separates those who thrive from those who falter?

Trust, Inc. is built upon the premise that an organization's greatest success will come about not despite the leader's values—but because of them. It is our experience, backed by the latest research, that organizations that place a high value on trust even in the face of adversity can count on players who are on the same page, who have the clarity and courage to address the real root problems and the confidence both to carry through on plans dutifully and to seek opportunities to innovate. As the organization learns to speak and act in alignment, the payoff is enhanced productivity.

Given the importance of trust in our lives, communities, companies and world, it is not surprising that two business executives who share a love of philosophy, psychology and organizational theory would have found their way quickly to this topic when introduced casually by a mutual friend. An added perk, however, is that both of us—who have become not only friends but co-authors—have had long, successful careers and work experience in multiple fields and under varying circumstances. This backs up our shared realization that there need be no discrepancy between personal values and organizational goals.

We don't just theorize about the alignment between trust and ethics as an abstract value. Each of us has had our own values tested in the day-to-day challenges of leading a team, a division, a company. For example, how do you address the issue of employee theft? Judith was faced with turning around the divisional culture of a well-respected company where the routine "borrowing" of pens and markers for home use cost the company and ultimately the consumer tens of thousands of dollars. How do you handle unpleasant information that is the public's right to know but that could cause the company distress, such as when one of Carol's public relations clients discovered an unacceptable level of nitrites in their leading food product, Italian dry salami? What do you do when you discover that otherwise excellent employees are padding their expense accounts, using illegally-obtained information for competitive advantage, making decisions that may be good for the company in the short-run but that will hurt others over time? You cannot have trust without ethics—nor can you have ethics without trust.

Whether providing direction to 20,000 direct reports at a multinational corporation or inspiring a team of 23 at a professional services firm, we have had to dig deep to find the key to the restoration of trust when faced with challenges such as these. We've often been confronted with making tough decisions requiring us to determine when and where to draw the ethical line. Sometimes, we've had to take leaps of faith, trusting that the right decision—though costly to ourselves or our company short-term—will pay off for all of us on multiple levels in the end. Overall, we have won more battles than we've lost, but we wear our hard-earned scars like badges of honor, having come to understand that the stakes of trust are high—and that they are worth fighting for.

In a world that prefers its issues to be black and white, the issue of trust carries with it all the complexities of life, itself. To respond adequately, we must become willing to dig deep beneath the surface, to uncover our own most deeply held values. We must also be willing to confront and transcend our biases, assumptions and personal preferences in order to provide equal and impartial consideration to those who challenge us with differing perspectives. Given the multiple influences that press upon us, we need to find a reliable way to sort through the input—as well as our own complicated responses to it. Ultimately, we must find the courage to do the right thing, no matter what.

We propose that building rather than breaching trust requires leaders to live and work in the largely uncharted territory that lies beyond compliance. This is the realm of character development, values clarification and above all, the ability to look beyond short-term gains to serve the greater good. In this realm, what separates those who thrive from those who falter is the willingness to trust, the wisdom to question and the courage to lead.

Who will benefit?

We wrote *Trust, Inc.* to be of particular assistance to business and organizational leaders who are charged with the responsibility for cultivating an ethical climate while running a competitive operation. These include CEOs, human resource professionals, public relations, financial and legal officers as well as internal and external management consultants. This is a time in history when a manager's testifying, "I never expected…" is no longer a valid excuse for ethical lapses. There is a pressing need for a practical tool for leaders who want to encourage employees at all levels to fully embrace organizational values.

We also reach out to educated individuals in the general public fascinated by the intellectual, political and personal ramifications of organizational trust and its relationship to business ethics. Finally, this book is a candidate for inclusion in business ethics and organizational leadership courses at all levels of higher education, especially at the undergraduate business major, MBA and Executive MBA levels. Alumni of even illustrious business schools and programs find themselves grappling for a solid foothold in an increasingly slippery ethical landscape. As the demand on higher education to provide practical guidance and resources for business leaders reaches a critical mass, this book is ready and willing to serve.

Book organization

In *Trust, Inc.*, the apparent gap between individual values and organizational goals is bridged by a series of self-assessments and learning exercises. The heart of the book is a four-step ethical decision-making process. Part One, "The New Accountability," lays the foundation for *Trust, Inc.*, grabbing the reader on multiple levels. After introducing the premise of the book, readers are guided through several self-assessment exercises designed to provide them with a deeper understanding of their personal values and ethical perspectives. They are then led to recognize the importance and pervasiveness of their relationship to trust, which operates, often invisibly, beneath the surface of everyday decisions and throughout organizational life.

After the basics have been established, readers explore the ramifications of their self-discovery. Rather than building trust as a matter of simply following rules—the "old accountability"—readers consider what it really takes to tackle the complexities of an ethical life. Included in the issues is the disconnection many people feel between their values at home and at work. We also address why disagreements arise with others over definitions of right and wrong, confusion about the difference between poor judgment and unethical behavior, and why it is that "feeling" that something is the right thing to do is not always a reliable indicator of what should be done in a given situation.

Part Two introduces a four-step decision-making process that guides the leader to address with honesty, clarity and courage the complex, challenging issues that arise daily. The four steps, which comprise the easy-to-remember acronym LEAP are: **L**earn everything you can, **E**valuate your options, **A**ccess your intuition and **P**ut your decision to the test. Each of these important action steps, critical to the advancement of the organization's reputation, comprises a chapter in section two.

Part Three, "Ethical Leadership", explicitly forges the alignment between individual values and organizational goals, including strategies that support the advancement of a culture that is most likely to deliver both ethical and bottom-line results. In this final section of three chapters, the authors consider cutting edge research drawn from psychology, sociology and management studies relating to the development of individual and organizational resilience. Subjects include the need for the creation of a meaningful worldview shared by individuals at all levels of the organization; the role and pitfalls of using intuition in decision-making; and the importance of establishing trust through communication, empathy and humor. In addition, *Trust, Inc.* prescribes what we call "a custodial chain of integrity" in which indications and root causes for ethical issues are addressed at an early stage, before they develop into full-fledged problems. Arguing that business has to be personal, *Trust, Inc.* provides the tools and motivation necessary to help leaders at all levels of organizational life bridge the gap between individual aspirations and the attainment of corporate goals.

Over cups of steaming tea, seated in noisy cafes and on deck chairs beneath overhanging trees, the two of us challenged ourselves to respond to the question *"Trust: how does one do that?"* In the pages following, we are grateful to have the opportunity to share our answer with you.

Judith Rogala and Carol Orsborn
Los Angeles, California

PART ONE

The New Accountability

How One Ought to Lead

———

Trust: How Does One "Do" That?

Faced with daily headlines trumpeting the embarrassing and destructive ramifications of breaches of trust, leaders are more motivated than ever to build an organization in which employees, clients and Wall Street can believe. But is it possible to build trust in the workplace and still guide one's organization to success through the compromising pressures, challenges and temptations of the contemporary marketplace? Not only is it possible, but *Trust, Inc.* argues that today's companies will achieve their greatest success not despite their leaders' emphasis on the cultivation of trust in organizational life—but because of it. This premise is supported by the latest research, which demonstrates that leading an organization worthy of respect can deliver tangible benefits to the bottom line.

The relationship between trust and profitability

There are multiple reasons for the positive relationship between the level of trust in a company and its profitability. On an organizational level, research shows that a culture based on such values as honesty, consistency and clarity reduces the costs associated with litigation, lobbying and regulation, not to mention savings related to the retention of crisis public relations services. On the proactive side, the ability of marketing departments to tell a story about a company in which they can be proud, builds trust with consumers, suppliers and others who can help advance the organization's goals. As an added benefit, the firmer a company's reputation for honesty, reliability and respect, the lower the turnover and the easier the recruitment. The reputation for proving worthy of trust also plays a critical role in the organization's relationship with the financial community, making or breaking its ability to access capital in times of need or opportunity.

The benefits are evident. But how, exactly, does one "do" trust? Many leaders complain that the values they practice in their personal lives outside of work just won't cut it in the pressured environment of today's global marketplace. Building a trustworthy organization can be difficult under the best of circumstances. But in times of intense societal change, such as our own, the challenges—and the stakes—are even higher. What does it mean to trust others in a global economy, for instance, where issues of conflicting loyalties, broken promises and divergent standards are fought out at the national, regional and even tribal levels? Even in traditional industries and fields, there are shifting rules and interpretations of the law on issues revolving around trust. In light of recent legislation, for instance, to whom do the lawyer and the accountant owe their loyalty? Is it to the client or to governmental agencies charged with the responsibility for oversight? Confidentialities, which were once kept as a testimony to the highest standards, are now vulnerable to being breached in the name of a greater good.

Many of us have personally witnessed the compelling and seductive forces that challenge a values-driven model of leadership, such as the one we propose in this book. Pressures on today's leaders include the tendency towards c-suite isolation and the "hoax management" of shortsighted greed associated with making the numbers. Employees, too, have pressures and temptations to overcome. Most pressing is their reluctance to buck a system that they believe rewards unethical behavior, especially if they perceive that their livelihood is at stake. No wonder so many consider there to be a crisis of confidence in business as an institution. It is tempting, in the climate of widespread mistrust and cynicism, to argue that ethical shortcuts, grabbing whatever one can for short-term gain, is justified.

Pressures and temptations

However, at the same time that many leaders succumb to the pressures of compromise, expediency, denial or self-delusion, others somehow find a way to rise above the challenges, temptations and pitfalls. They lead their organizations to reap the rewards of becoming internationally respected for their values. These are companies that can be counted upon to keep their promises. From supplier to CEO to Chairman of the Board, there is a custodial chain of integrity that will not be breached.

What separates organizations that thrive from those that falter? In the wake of legislation intended to encourage ethical actions and to punish indiscretion, most notably the recent enactment of the Sarbanes-Oxley Act, it is tempting to think that the answer relies simply on "compliance." But is following the letter of the law enough? Continuing breaches of trust lead a growing number of concerned business leaders, ethics academics and the general public to suggest the answer is, "No." More and more organizational leaders are realizing that accountability alone as a reaction to external pressures is unlikely to make ethical conviction the personal and organizational norm, rather than an exception.

Rather, it is becoming increasingly apparent that individuals and organizations that can be counted upon to merit their stakeholders' trust, share traits of trust as well as resilience. When greeted with obstacles, resilient leaders know that plunging through to the depths of challenges is where "how one ought to lead" can be found.

Happily, moral proficiency is something that can be cultivated. Arguing that business has to be personal, we contend that it is the leader's responsibility to flow his or her ethics through the company, setting the standard to which all levels of organizational life will aspire. Research shows clearly that employees prefer to work in a consistently ethical environment, instinctively telling the difference between a company that gives integrity lip service and a company "that really means it." Organizations that thrive ethically even in the face of adversity trust that all the players are on the same page, that real root problems are addressed, all pertinent details attended to. The pay off is enhanced productivity. As the organization learns to speak and act in alignment, the most powerful words are: "I knew what I had to do would be okay with you."

The latest research

The guidance on the pages that follow is consistent with the latest business ethics scholarship for application in real world situations. *Managing Ethics in Business Organizations* (Stanford Business Books, 2003) includes findings that are consistent with our premise. Based on multiple sources of data, including interviews with hundreds of ethics officers from a who's who of major corporations, scholars Linda Klebe Trevino and Gary R. Weaver's work represents the definitive summary of leading edge business ethics research. Among the areas covered is the one most closely related to our own area of inquiry: the impact of values-based ethical training programs on employee morale. Summarizing research, Trevino and Weaver report: "Employees' reactions to such programs are influenced by their perceptions of how fairly the organization treats them. In short, when the program signals that the company is concerned about the employee, not merely looking to protect the company or its officers from harm, desirable ethics program outcomes (such as reduced unethical behavior) are more likely."

Not surprisingly, the research reveals employee preference for values-based over compliance-centered training tools and resources. Employees report that ethics programs that focus solely on the detection and discipline of transgressions suggest that employees are not to be trusted. A values-oriented program, on the other hand, is perceived as acknowledging that employees are already committed to ethical behavior. "The task of the program is to encourage the development of meaningful, shared ethical values within the organization's particular context," Trevino and Weaver write, summarizing some of the pertinent studies. "In a values-oriented program, emphasis is on activities that aid employees in decision-making, provide ethical advice and counseling, and support the development of a consensus about what constitutes good business ethics… A strong values orientation, then, supports employee aspirations and suggests that the organization embodies a collective commitment that applies equally to all persons." This is but one of the findings that will, over the next several years, be extending its influence from academia to corporate leaders faced with the everyday pressures and responsibilities of the workplace.

This is how ethical organizations are built, with organizational leaders working towards the establishment of trusting relationships with multiple stakeholders, one decision at a time. By following the principles in this book, the values-driven leader will learn how to "do" trust, creating the organizational culture most likely to succeed on every level—and under any circumstance.

Name Your Values

Several nights ago, we were invited to a gathering of successful businesspeople and professionals, hosted by a prominent corporate consultant. Chatting our way around the room, we were able to catch bits of conversation. A seasoned stock analyst shared a life's worth of wisdom with a younger real estate associate, straining eagerly across a full plate of hors d'oeuvres to catch every word.

"If you want to succeed, don't trust anyone. Always watch out for number one." Elsewhere, an advertising industry executive and her boss were toasting each other about that day's big win.

"You took a big leap of faith putting your trust in me to lead that pitch."

"I knew you had it in you," the other responded. "I've built this agency on trust."

Taking some well-earned "r and r" in this cozy environment, many of these businesspeople—had they been challenged—would have simply believed they were telling the "truth." Without thinking, we adopt and act on assumptions we believe to be universally accepted as the way things really are. Whose truth will prevail only becomes an issue when the hard-nosed stock analyst and the trusting advertising president get seated side by side at dinner. By dessert, one thinks the other is an insensitive jerk—the second thinks the other is a gullible sap. Happily, the most difficult decision the two needed to make together that evening was who gets first choice out of the breadbasket.

Competing truths

We are not always so lucky. In our diverse workplaces operating at warp speed in an increasingly global economy, we can no longer take for granted that we share our value systems and beliefs with every significant other. Even if you are fortunate enough to know that your individual ethics are in alignment with those espoused by your company, are you really on the same page with the client who believes that this is a dog-eat-dog world? How about the supplier who "has to make a living" by reneging on your agreed-upon price? What do you do when a foreign partner explains that "this is the way we do business here," be it bribes or lying, knowing full well that what is being suggested is anything but ethical? And then, too, there are those times when even you aren't sure whether what you believe is the right thing to do.

Not only do we not always agree on what ethical behavior is, we do not even know if we agree on what the word means. What do you think of when you see the word "ethics?" Is it about the rules—as in complying with federal regulations? Is it about commandments—as in following the dictates of a higher, spiritual authority? For some, the word carries with it memories of the philosophy class you struggled with (or aced); for others, it's today's headlines with the political and economic ramifications of this or that moral transgression. If the very word "ethics" brings up so many different interpretations and feelings, how can we ever hope to get on the same page in terms of what it means to be an ethical individual, let alone an ethical organization? If we cannot hope to agree on what ethics is, how can we begin building trust that we are on the same page in terms of our expectations and aspirations?

Ethics defined

Let us suggest one definition that will at least give us a place to start, one broad enough to encompass all the possibilities. We like the ancient Greek approach to the question, "How ought we to live?" Building upon this, we have taken the liberty of proposing that ethics in the business context could best be defined as no less a matter than "How ought we to lead?" This deceptively simple question assumes an ability to process multiple possibilities, influences and considerations in order to arrive at a satisfactory answer, suitable, at the very least, for your own personal use. Another name for this process, whether carried out with or without conscious reflection, would be common sense. This book assumes that you do, indeed, have common sense—and that you live an essentially good life.

The study of ethics goes one step further: it provides you with a structured way to process multiple inputs and influences, internal and external, so that when you do find yourself treading on issues that put you on treacherous terrain, you will have at least two fewer variables with which to deal. Certainty number one: you will come to know where you stand in regard to your own values and beliefs. Certainty number two: you will have a way to think things through when you are confronted with differing values and beliefs. With just these two certainties in place, you can learn how to negotiate your way deliberately through the competing values operating, often invisibly, beneath the surface of everyday decisions and throughout organizational life. This is particularly timely, given the growing resistance by the media, the shareholders, the public and the courts to the leader's heartfelt declaration, "I never expected that this could happen in my organization…" as a legitimate excuse for ethical lapses.

Beyond compliance

By now, you have probably already come to realize that this particular approach to ethics is not simply about following rules. In the wake of legislation intended to encourage ethical actions and to punish indiscretion, it is tempting to think that knowing right from wrong relies simply on "compliance." Of course, knowing the laws and regulations are an important place to begin. But is following the letter of the law enough? It is becoming increasingly obvious that building in accountability primarily as a reaction to external pressures is unlikely to produce the level of commitment necessary to make ethical behavior a habit. And even if we did have the will to be ethical in the realm beyond compliance, what separates those who thrive from those who falter is the realization that right and wrong is neither always simple nor uncontroversial, not even for the majority of people in business who are well intentioned.

Entry through values

If we do not propose to provide you with a set of rules, where do we begin? We propose that you enter through the portal of your own personal values. Mythologist Joseph Campbell, conversing with Bill Moyers in their book *The Power of Myth* suggested that our values and beliefs are like computer software. You enter the data and the computer responds according to your commands. Our programs include the understanding of the world in which we were born and raised, but over time, we have many opportunities to "play with the software." Our belief systems grow and change over time, although it is likely that for most of us, at least some of our early influences continue to be a presence in the programming of our lives. Whether it be a big issue—such as whether or not to take the compensation package offered, knowing that the organization has yet to turn a profit, or a micro-issue—such as who gets first choice out of the breadbasket, there is a direct link between the nature of your values and the quality of your decisions. This is particularly true at those times when the demands of the moment press upon you to make a split-second decision. It is at those times—whether pressed or not—when people may be hurt, deceived, or treated unfairly.

As big as this is, this is just the beginning. For when individuals know what their values are and experience an alignment between their personal ethics and corporate goals, there is an unexpected benefit. Alignment around core values allows leaders at all levels of the organization to speak and act in a kind of ethical shorthand. Inefficiencies are lessened, employee motivation heightened. Organizations that thrive ethically even in the face of adversity trust that all the players are on the same page, that the real root problems are addressed, all pertinent details attended to. The pay off is enhanced productivity, with individuals at all levels of organizational life feeling pride in their place of employment. This experience of going to work could be like that of Judith and her division of 20,000 at Federal Express. "The saying was that we were willing to bleed purple for FedEx—the color of our logo. There was that much loyalty and unity." If this has not yet been your experience, it may take something of a leap of faith to pay heed to the underlying premise of our approach to ethics: that your greatest success will come not despite your most deeply-held values—but because of them.

Name your values

So, before seeing just exactly how you can put your values to work, the first important step is to bring to light your own personal values. What are the cultural inheritances, family and social dynamics and belief systems that formed your ethical perspective on how you think life and work ought to be? Access to this information is easier than you might imagine. All you need to know is your name. The name you use in your daily life is an open book, revealing the influences and dynamics that have been acting upon you since birth. While you may still use the name you were given at birth, many of us have a long history of personal names—an evolutionary record of decisions made, milestones passed and values embodied. Names can pay homage to honored ancestors, family trades and legacies, marriages made and broken and much, much more. For example, do you know Ed Hillary? That wasn't the name on his birth certificate…but it was the name of a New Zealand beekeeper who loved physical challenges. Ed thought of himself as a simple man—an adventurer and athlete who loved the challenge of climbing to the peak of the highest mountains he could find. It was as Ed that he became the first man to make it to the summit of Mount Everest—but it was as Sir Edmund Hillary that he descended into his new life as one of the most famous men in the world. At first, the name that was given to him by Queen Elizabeth II seemed to be a terrible burden, bearing more responsibility than he cared to or felt capable of handling. But over time, he grew into it. In fact, Sir Hillary became an elder statesman and diplomat, internationally respected for his ambitious and innovative aid program to the people of Nepal.

We don't need to be knighted to have our name exert (or reflect) the influences upon us. Even individuals with only their original name can learn much about themselves in the process, for retaining the name you were given at birth—against all the pressures and influences that press upon us over time—tells a story, as well. Shall we begin?

What's in a Name? A Self-Assessment

Begin by making a list of all the names you have been given and used from the time of your birth to present day. Carol's list is eight names long, with her first name the only constant in a lifetime of negotiations with external and internal influences. Starting as Carol Linn Matzkin and ending with Dr. Carol Orsborn, her personal history of names reflects both constant and developing values related to marriage, her religion and her family of origin, and her professional attainments. Recently guiding her classroom of doctoral students in organizational leadership through this exercise inspired by one of her clients, Carol's group of twenty students produced an astonishing aggregate of over 100 names. Several class members talked of the emotional linkage (pride or rejection) to saint namesakes, a loaded package of values given to them by the Catholic Church. In other cases, complicated names had been altered or dropped for the sake of efficiency. Some had clung to original names out of a sense of loyalty, some out of laziness. Based on the student's place of origin, names took on added dimensions of significance. Some cultures carry the parent's name or trade, bespeaking an on-going intimacy between the generations. In others, such as a number of Native American cultures, the community considers the individual's special relationship to an aspect of nature as the source for a name change at adolescence, part of a tribal rite of passage. For one member of the class, genealogical research had revealed an ancestral name that was changed for political and social reasons at Ellis Island. The speaker was near tears as she told of the courageous stand she had taken to legally change her Americanized name back to the original.

The values that influence you

You, too, may be prompted through this exercise to remember, recognize or learn anew about the values that energize you. Who gave you your name? Does your original name tell you something about the influences and expectations placed upon you by others? Were there role models you were meant to emulate? While we are given names at birth, the choices we make along the way modify, affirm or resist our original values. As you make your list, ask yourself when and why you began making or resisting changes in your name. Even if you didn't change your name legally, were you ever given a nickname? Did you have the urge to change your name in response to pressures at school? If you married, did that alter your name? What does it say about you if/whether and when you chose to take, modify or drop one name or another? What does the name you use today tell you about where you've come from, about your take on how you ought to live?

The values continuum

After you've made your list of names, take a step back to seek out underlying themes related to the values that have come into play during the course of your life. To help you along, here is a list of values, paired to reflect the dynamic tension between divergent tendencies. In each pair, think about where you fall on the continuum between extremes. Circle the number that reflects your experience. Five is highest, one is lowest. Feel free to think of additional pairings particular to your own life story.

Loyal	5	4	3	2	1	0	1	2	3	4	5	Self-Serving
Domineering	5	4	3	2	1	0	1	2	3	4	5	Collaborating
Industrious	5	4	3	2	1	0	1	2	3	4	5	Laid-back
Responsible	5	4	3	2	1	0	1	2	3	4	5	Carefree
Suspicious	5	4	3	2	1	0	1	2	3	4	5	Trusting
Cautious	5	4	3	2	1	0	1	2	3	4	5	Risk-taking
Self-first	5	4	3	2	1	0	1	2	3	4	5	Others first
Duplicitous	5	4	3	2	1	0	1	2	3	4	5	Honest
Respectful	5	4	3	2	1	0	1	2	3	4	5	Non-deferential
Arrogant	5	4	3	2	1	0	1	2	3	4	5	Humble
Judgmental	5	4	3	2	1	0	1	2	3	4	5	Tolerant
Supportive	5	4	3	2	1	0	1	2	3	4	5	Assertive
Pushing	5	4	3	2	1	0	1	2	3	4	5	Patient
Desperate	5	4	3	2	1	0	1	2	3	4	5	Confident
Straightforward	5	4	3	2	1	0	1	2	3	4	5	Rationalizing
Hypocritical	5	4	3	2	1	0	1	2	3	4	5	Genuine
Grateful	5	4	3	2	1	0	1	2	3	4	5	Greedy

What we learn

Most of the students in the class discovered for themselves two important things. The first is that they were, indeed, born into this life with a particular worldview and set of values waiting for them. The second is that they had many opportunities to reinforce, question and in some cases discard aspects of their values over time. Some of the changes were advancements, providing the individual with a heightened sense of integrity: a unity between developing values and public identity. Others felt that they had made mistakes along the way that had already been or could yet be rectified. The bottom line is that our values, while continuing to be in on-going conversation with our original programming, are also works in progress. This insight provides us with all the ammunition we need to refute individuals like the dean at a major university's prestigious business school who recently resisted the faculty's push to require a course in ethics to be taken by MBAs. His reason? "If they weren't taught it at home, they sure as heck won't learn it now."

One species or two?

In truth, by neglecting to offer ethics classes to business school students, generations of business leaders—including many of those who have recently traded the c-suite for a corner pen with bars—are given the message that the corporation's needs are best served by having one set of values for your personal life, and a separate set at work.

Mohanbir Sawhney, McCormick Tribune professor of technology at Northwestern University's Kellogg School of Management, tells the story of a Freudian slip observed on a sign at the reception desk of a major corporation: "Please leave your values at the desk. Management is not responsible for losses."

Obviously, if you hope to align your personal ethics with those of your organization, you've got to know what your company's values are. We're not just talking lip service, here, but the real values operating, often invisibly, beneath the surface that inspire, influence or warp your work community's notion of how you ought to lead. You have probably already figured out that you can't always trust that what an organization claims as their values publicly is what is actually going on in that company below the surface. Of course, it's a good start to have a written code of honor, mission statements, sensitivity trainings and the like. But what really happens when doing the right thing and maximizing profitability in the short-term appear to be at odds? How about issues of personal power versus the greater good?

The fact is, you already know more than you think about your organization's worldview. In fact, this would be an opportune time to revisit the values continuum of contrasting pairs, this time completing the exercise on behalf of your organization. Where are you and your organization aligned? Where are the gaps?

Bridging the gaps

Our approach to ethics is based on the premise that human beings—even human beings in pinstriped suits—are more effective, more motivated and dare we say it, happier if they have but one set of values that works both at home and at the office. In every company that Judith leads, she tells her employees that there is no such thing as business ethics. There's only ethics.

Nevertheless, so many of us find ourselves and our organizations—let alone suppliers, customers and investors—split into two species instead of one. Quoting author M. Scott Peck, the two species are "Homo Sapiens" (humans who think) and "Homo Economicus" (humans who think but primarily about the size of their compensation packages). The split occurs when we allow pressures and temptations to override our own good common sense. Just as we have seen that values can change for the better, so is it sadly true that values can be subverted to serve any one of a number of masters: greed, expediency, status concerns and laziness, among them.

The erosion of values

The oddest thing is that we are not always aware when our innate, good values have become eroded and values that would turn our own stomachs, if we stopped long enough to think about it, have come to take their place. In discussing the downfall of Enron, one commentator suggested that excess of almost any kind corrupts even good intentions. With Enron, that excess was something normally associated with a positive virtue—the passion to innovate. Even innovation, however, can become too clever for its own good. At an annual meeting of the Society for Business Ethics, not-yet-yellowed pamphlets containing Kenneth Lay's article "What Should a CEO Expect from a Board?" were being given away as wry souvenirs of just how wrong things can go. Prominent in the verbiage is Enron's emphasis on "the qualities of strength of character, an inquiring and independent mind, practical wisdom and mature judgment." In a later chapter, we will talk more about the organizational pressures that subvert individual as well as organizational values. At this juncture, it is worthwhile noting that moral lapses are not always conscious or deliberate. As the psychologist Abraham Maslow is reported to have said: "Most people aren't evil—they're just schlemiels." There is, in other words, a difference between immoral behavior and just plain poor judgment. That line usually has to do with intent, namely whether and to what degree issues of personal gain are consciously engaged.

Some transgressions, while nevertheless demanding to be addressed appropriately, are relatively benign. While Judith ran the Midwestern and Canadian divisions for Federal Express, for instance, she quickly recognized that the amount of money going for pens, markers and papers, was out of line. Upon investigation, she discovered that employees were inadvertently taking office supplies home, and they never quite made it back to work. Often, these supplies found their way into home offices for use both on official and personal business matters, into children's school projects and into neglected corners where they languished unnoticed for days, months or years. Most would have been horrified if they'd realized that what they were doing was essentially stealing company resources. Division leadership decided that what was required to rectify this situation was not punishment but amnesty. Soon, empty barrels set up in strategic locations were filled to the brim—a savings to the company of many thousands of dollars. The value of the message in terms of employee morale: priceless.

Ethical transgressions are not always so easily rectified, consciences so handily cleared. There are those who cross the line between thoughtlessness and conscious intent, rationalizing their greed, hypocrisy and dishonesty with all manner of excuses. We have all known someone who felt it perfectly legitimate to pad expense accounts to compensate for what was felt to be a lower salary than one deserved. Another takes or offers bribes "because that's the way it's done in our industry." Especially when lodged within corporate cultures where values messages are weak, ambivalent or even openly supportive of unethical behavior. Some—who would be appalled by lying, stealing or cheating in their personal relationships—cross over the line seemingly without effort or thought. It is like the story about the crab and the boiling pot of water. As one folk legend goes, if you put a certain kind of crab into the water while it is at full boil, the crab jumps right back out. If you put the crab into the water while it is cool, however, the crab just settles right in, ending up as a steaming bowl of crab soup. Without conscious awareness of both your and your organization's values, you can easily get used to life in a boiling pot of eroded values. In fact, be thankful if you have the capacity to feel guilt. That means that when you do cross the lines between personal values, poor judgment and unethical behavior, even you don't buy your rationalizations.

In later chapters, we will offer specific advice on how leadership can help employees at all levels of organizational life close the gap between individual and organizational values. For the time being, however, let us act as if you already work for a company that really means it. Even so, the reality is that even in the best division or company—not to mention the larger community of relationships that define your everyday life at work—disagreements over values will arise. What then?

Measure the Golden Rule

When we talk about ethical challenges, we are not only addressing situations where someone chooses to do right and another someone chooses to do wrong when there is clearly a right and a wrong thing to do. Nor are we speaking only about those times when an individual departs from a group norm in willful disregard of organizational standards. This chapter addresses the most difficult ethical dilemma of all: the situation of right versus right, where principled individuals with arguably valid moral positions come down on different sides of an issue.

Two versions of justice

As an example, one of the hats Judith wore at TWA was serving on the management team responsible for labor relations. TWA had instituted a zero tolerance policy for stealing. The policy was an attempt to eliminate debates concerning where to draw the line when it came to "borrowing" company property. Everybody knows it's stealing when a $10,000 power tool somehow finds its way into an airplane mechanic's home workshop. But was it stealing for an airplane maintenance person to take home an unopened can of soda left at flight's end that had been left on a customer's seat? And now, what if the employee is a long-term veteran of the company with an otherwise stellar record? The zero tolerance policy eliminated what Judith considered to be the slippery slope of exceptions to the rule with its potential for elitism, favoritism and confusion. On her watch, Judith decided that in the name of justice born of fairness and equality, the zero tolerance policy would be strictly enforced. Everybody in the company—pilot or machinist, with the company one month or several decades—would know where he or she stood and what the consequences would be. In fact, it was Judith's experience—substantiated later by her experiences at FedEx—that above all, people are looking for fair and consistent handling.

And then came a test. A 30-year-veteran making a basic living wage stole a minor item and was written up by management with the severity of punishment to be decided. Union and management went into arbitration over the issue. Against Judith's counsel, management acceded to union demands to alter policy to include seniority as a mitigating consideration. The worker was lightly reprimanded and reinstated. Ironically, from the union's perspective, this was also a victory for justice. To this day, Judith shakes her head over their position. "It sent such a terrible message: That it's okay to steal if you've been with us a long time. What were they thinking?"

Divergent values

In the best division or company—not to mention the larger community of relationships that define our everyday lives at work— even good people can disagree about what is the right thing to do in a particular circumstance. By Judith's own reckoning, the union people were well-meaning people as committed to doing what they believed to be the right thing as she was. In terms of this particular situation, she and they found themselves at opposite poles on the issue, each with a compelling argument formed by divergent values, beliefs and positional perspectives.

When disagreements do arise, it is natural for the first response to be an emotional one. Everybody feels that he or she knows best what should be done. In the heat of the moment, the manager takes action, only in hindsight manufacturing a rational explanation to "prove up" what he or she has done. People get upset, they vent, they rant. However, ethics is more than simply a matter of feeling that you know what the right thing to do is. If this were not the case, even good people would inevitably find themselves on opposite ledges of an ethical divide, their only recourse being to scream louder across the abyss than others who are equally passionate about their positions. The alternative, paying serious heed to others with whom we may profoundly disagree, seems impossibly complicated. Clearly, given the complexity inherent in many ethical dilemmas, the urge to simplify is virtually irresistible. We yearn for a universal approach that can be counted upon to help us make the best decisions for all concerned. Ergo: The Golden Rule.

The Golden Rule

The Golden Rule is a prime candidate for the job, making appearances in cultures and religions around the world and through history. In contemporary America, we tend to think of The Golden Rule using biblical language: "Do unto others as you would have others do unto you." But this is one version among many. In Confucianism, we are told "What you do not like when done to yourself, do not do to others," and in Hinduism, "Let no man do to another what would be repugnant to himself." Even a beloved Nigerian proverb gets the message across: "One going to take a pointed stick to pinch a baby bird should first try it on himself to feel how it hurts."

The thing about the Golden Rule is this: It works beautifully when practiced within a shared and coherent value system. The CEO establishes the principle that a zero tolerance policy against stealing should be applied fairly and equally across the board, for instance. In such an environment, the leader would not expect others to steal from the company—whether he or she has been with the company six days or thirty years. Everybody is on the same page. The transgressor is fired, be it a pilot or a mechanic, $1 or $100,000, six days or thirty years. The Golden Rule works. Case closed. The Golden Rule works equally well, by the way, if everybody from the CEO on down believes that if someone were to steal something minor after many years of faithful service, we should forgive him or her as we ourselves would expect to be forgiven. Same Golden Rule, different interpretation.

A worthy goal

The elegance of the Golden Rule when individuals in an organization are on the same page is, in fact, the point of this book. To serve as an ethical leader, you need to be willing to do everything within your power to articulate ethical values, both within your organization and to your various external constituencies: your Boards of Directors, community, suppliers, clients and customers. You need to make your organization's moral stances explicit, hiring and establishing relationships on the basis of individuals knowing and buying into your organization's values. You need to model and reinforce your moral point of view, addressing and resolving differences through conversation and training on an on-going basis—not just in the heat of an ethical crisis. Above all, there needs to be alignment between what you say and what you do. The goal of ethical leadership, in fact, is to aim to be the kind of organization where the Golden Rule works: an ethical shorthand that promises consistency on the part of the leader. As a result, the environment exists for an interconnected web of individuals working together to move ahead as quickly and efficiently as possible under all circumstances, knowing what is expected of everyone without having to ask. This may sound utopian. But it is not an impossible dream. As the Golden Rule's universality indicates, we share a lot. In fact, the deeper we look, the more values we find we have in common. We all want our opinions to be taken seriously, for example. We want to trust that others mean what they say. We want what is special or unique about us to be respected. We want others to keep an open mind and we want to think of ourselves as fair and just.

Research points up the notion of shared values. Psychologist Milton Rokeach developed the most widely used system to rate and rank the importance of values to an individual or group. Based on the Rokeach values survey, 91 American CEOs representing 57 industries rated a sense of accomplishment, family security and self-respect as the top three values reflecting their lifelong aspirations. Other values that made it high up on the list included happiness and freedom. Shared values can also cross national borders. In a study of 15,000 managers, it was found that executives in Europe, the U.S. and Australia most admire superiors who are honest, forward-looking, inspiring, and competent. In the pages to come, we will address the ways and means to identify and address these deeply held values. But in the shallows where most of us live most of the time, it is a big mistake to make the assumption that we are all the same. And even more dangerous: to make the mistake of believing that how you would like to be treated is automatically how others would like to be treated, as well.

Theories differ, too

You have begun the journey to ethical proficiency in the previous chapter by getting a grip on the moral ground upon which you stand: the values that formed you. Now it is time to continue this journey, coming to understand that not only your values—but, in fact, your very sense of the world—is not something that is necessarily shared with every conversation partner. Unless you consider yourself to be a philosopher, you have probably not had or taken the time to articulate for yourself what your beliefs about the world may be—let alone put into words the equally pervasive but differing perspectives of others. At the same time, however, these subconsciously held positions determine not only how you will come to the ethical decision-making table—but how you will approach virtually every issue that crosses your path.

Philosophers are professional thinkers who try to make sense of all this. In fact, their theories delineate the major ethical points of view people tend to take. While there are nearly as many variations on these themes as there are people on our planet, the following Ethical Assessment will help you recognize not only your own personal theoretical orientation, but the potentially divergent positions of conversation and negotiating partners, as well. Be as honest and thoughtful as you can as you pick the responses that come closest to your own. Don't worry about inconsistencies or about what your answers might reveal about you. The critical issue here is not whether your point of view is the right or even "best" one—but that thoughtful people can hold different points of view.

ETHICAL ASSESSMENT

Circle the statements below that complete the sentence most accurately for you. Then add up the number of a's through g's. If two or more answers seem to be of equal value to you, you can make note of multiple letters.

1. When I'm trying to figure out what the right thing to do is…
a. I look at the particular situation and come up with a solution that will work best for that time, place and context.
b. I turn to my religion or faith for guidance.
c. I think about what is best for me.
d. I do unto others as I would have them do unto me.
e. I consider my motivation, believing that it is important to do the right thing for the right reason.
f. I consider everybody's rights to be equally important.
g. I trust myself to come from my highest ethical aspirations.

2. In regards to judging other people's ethical behavior…
a. Nobody has the right to intervene in deciding what is right or wrong for somebody else.
b. It is important to test what they are doing against what divine law has told us is right and wrong.
c. You can trust that they are just doing whatever is most likely to advance their own self-interest.
d. Take only into account what they do rather than whatever their motivation may be.
e. Give them credit for trying to do the right thing, even if it has bad results.
f. Everyone has certain inalienable rights.
g. It is important to be both compassionate and just.

3. In terms of what it means to live "the good life"…

a. It's a waste of time to try to define this as any one thing for all people.

b. How my religion or organized belief system teaches it is literally true.

c. How I define this will be completely determined by my environment, family and other influences.

d. The consequences of my actions are far more important than my motivations.

e. Being motivated to do the right thing, regardless of the consequences, is the key to happiness.

f. I can do whatever I please short of violating another's rights.

g. Without virtue, the good life would not be possible.

4. Knowing what is the right thing to do in a particular circumstance…

a. Depends upon the expectations of my culture.

b. Is what a higher power is telling me to do.

c. Is about taking care of my own needs and interests.

d. Asks me to determine what will be best for everyone.

e. Revolves around what must be done because it is my duty.

f. Must not impinge on other people's rights.

g. Has to do with my basic character: the kind of person I am.

Number

a. _____

b. _____

c. _____

d. _____

e. _____

f. _____

g. _____

Interpretation

If you haven't studied philosophical theory since graduating school—or if you've never taken a formal course in ethics—you may be surprised that not only do your answers tend to group around one letter or another, but that the letters are each associated with a formal philosophical school of thought. Don't feel neglected, by the way, if your answers were scattered between several or even all categories. There's a theory for you, too.

Mostly a's

You instinctively understand the complexities of our times and question your right to make value judgments about others. You tend to believe that people ought to be free to do whatever it is they want, as long as nobody gets hurt. The strength of this position is that your theory matches the diversity of opinions, positions and beliefs that confront us on a daily basis. The weakness is that the quest to set standards for others and find common moral ground is usually relegated to the back burner, or abandoned entirely. Philosophers would call you a "relativist."

Mostly b's

Your religious and/or spiritual beliefs are fundamental to your ethical decision-making process. You believe that there is an objective, external source for determining right and wrong and that this knowledge is something that you and all others can access through faith. The strength of this position is that you have certainty about where you stand in regards to ethical judgments. The weakness is that you may be confronted with individuals who have been guided to arrive at different judgments, equally certain about the veracity of their source. You would be referred to as a "divine command theorist."

Mostly c's

You are someone who considers yourself to be a "realist." By that, you mean to say that all people put their self-interest above all else and that those who believe otherwise are just fooling themselves. This does not mean that you will never do good things for other people—but it does mean that you believe that you are doing so only because doing good things for others gives you a sense of personal satisfaction. The strength of this position is that it allows you to make decisions based on data that recognizes the darker shades of human nature, such as selfishness and greed. The weakness is that it does not acknowledge let alone encourage you or others to value self-sacrifice in service of a greater good. You would be considered an "ethical egoist."

Mostly d's

You believe that it is your job to make the sincere effort to do the greatest good for the greatest number of people. You are less interested in motivations and more interested in consequences, willing to do the right thing for the wrong reason if in the end, you will do more good than harm. The strength of this position is that you can utilize logic and rational processes, strategically and methodically weighing and balancing alternatives to make a decision you can feel good about. The weakness is that you may neglect to consider whether others who will be impacted by your decision share your definition of goodness. And concerning others, what about the equally valid needs, rights and desires of those who are not part of the "greatest number?" Do we not have an obligation also to consider the interests of the minority? You would be referred to as "utilitarian"— one who believes in the greatest good for the greatest number.

Mostly e's

You are less concerned with the results of your decision than you are with doing things for the right reasons. For you, good intentions are foremost, even if you may suffer for taking a firm ethical stance. You believe that we all have the moral obligation to make our decisions based on universal truths accessed through our consciences. The strength of this position is that you believe that it is possible for human beings to make judgments for themselves and for others concerning what is right and wrong. In fact, there will be consistency because what is right for one is right for everybody under all circumstances. The weakness is that this approach can be rigid, making it difficult to justify exceptions born of compassion or unique circumstances. You would be considered to be a "deontologist." Derived from the Greek word deon, meaning duty, a deontologist feels an obligation to do the right thing.

Mostly f's

Like the founding fathers of America, you believe that individuals have certain inalienable rights. You respect the rights of others and want to be left free to lay claim to your own rights, as well. You may perceive your ethical obligation to others as entailing a passive restraint from interference. Or you may be an activist, proactively helping others exercise their rights. The strength of your position is that you will have a core of clearly defined values upon which to base ethical decisions. The weakness of your position is that you may disagree with others about who gets to define the nature of those rights and in our increasingly pluralistic community, if, whether and how to determine to whom they should apply. You are a "rights theorist."

Mostly g's

You believe that the practice of ethics is based not on your actions or results, but on the basis of your character. You have defined certain virtues that you make the effort to cultivate in yourself and others. You believe that your greatest happiness comes about as a by-product of the nurturing of the highest expression of your human potential. The strength of this position is that you may achieve a consistency between who you are and the stances you take. The weakness is that you may be susceptible to evangelistic fervor, setting yourself up not only to judge other people's results, but their characters and intent. You are what the ancient Greek philosophers would have called a "virtue ethicist."

If your answers were all over the board...

You believe that different situations call for different theoretical responses. You may use utilitarianism in one context and rights theory in another—or even a combination of theories applied to a single situation, drawing insight and value from each. The strength of your position is that you can be flexible, apt to find common ground with discussion and negotiation partners, whatever the source of their point of view. The weakness is that you may relinquish your right to judge others, passively allowing indifference to be exercised in the name of tolerance. You would be referred to as an "ethical pluralist."

An ethical lens

Your philosophical orientation is the lens through which you view the ethical issues that arise in organizational life. You are likely to think of your view of the world as the truth—but it is important to note that every one of the points of view that has been described is based on a set of assumptions, preferences and convictions operating invisibly but pervasively in your everyday life. Each position, at its worst, can easily degenerate into bias, prejudice and even intolerance. Taken at their best, however, our differing philosophical orientations bring particular insights and perspectives to the ethical conversation. This exercise not only makes visible the various lenses through which morality is viewed, but leads us to recognize the distances that exist between the positions to be traversed so that, at the very least, we can know how far between us there is yet to go.

But what, then, is the destination? We envision a place where the Golden Rule actually works. When we arrive, it will be because ethical leaders have taken the time and done the hard work of telling the truth about both our individual and organizational values as well as our theoretical strengths and our weaknesses. As the following chapters prescribe, we will have learned how to cultivate an environment of mutual respect, providing equal and impartial consideration of all pertinent points of view. When we differ, we will have found the way to bring and elicit the best rather than the worst each of our positions has to offer. At the same time, we will have strengthened our conviction that the deeper we go, the more we will find what we have in common. As ethical leaders, we will come to stand for something that others in our organizations admire, and to which they aspire, building upon our shared values to provide courageous ethical leadership.

But the way can be long and hard, especially since the distance is not always only between yourself and others with whom you disagree. Sometimes, the greater abyss is between the stances you have taken and your own highest ethical aspirations. To close the gap between where you are and where you suspect you ought to be, you must find the means and courage to surface your most resolute biases, prejudices and opinions—only then to become willing to set them aside instantly, to be fair and objective in your judgments and decisions. You may have to make tough calls, overriding your own comfort or even your preferences in order to do the best, right thing. You may have to shed light on the intrigues of others, as well as your own, finding the strength to confront that which prefers to remain invisible.

We begin now to understand the true dimensions of ethical leadership. This is not something that can be found in the shallows of human interaction—emotionalism, prejudice and rationalization—but in the depths, where the productive work of ethical decision-making truly transpires.

CHAPTER FOUR

Solve the Real Problem

The last chapter established that ethical behavior requires something more of you than just feeling that you know the right thing to do in any given situation. But what we have not yet told you is that the *something more* is not just that you may have to negotiate with others who are just as passionate about their position. It is not just that you may be torn between compelling arguments pro and con.

Of course it is important to bring thoughtful consideration to these and many more of the issues already addressed. However, all the great values in the world won't mean a thing if what you are doing is trying to solve the wrong problem.

Root causes

You heard us right. Much of the time, the ethical challenge with which you are faced is not the real problem that needs to be resolved but rather, a symptom of a deeper issue that has put down roots somewhere in your organizational life. This does not mean that if you address only the surface issue as it has presented itself you can't satisfy legal requirements and sleep easy at night, honestly believing that you have done your best. It does mean, however, that unless you dig deeper to address the root causes, whatever went wrong in the first place is likely to go wrong again. Another unhappy rule of thumb: when it goes wrong next time, it will be worse.

What happened at TWA during Judith's tenure as a senior executive is an apt example. One of the managers had been caught padding his expense reports. The individual was submitted to corporate discipline—in this case, removed from the company entirely—and everybody moved on. But in Judith's view, this was not just an isolated incident. It was Act Two in a drama-already-in-progress that exposed an underlying pattern of ethical vulnerability operating beneath the surface of organizational life.

What was Act One? At the time, TWA—along with most of the

airline industry—had hit a slippery patch on the financial runway. The executive committee decided that the most efficient way to close the budget gap was to cut management salaries across the board. The members of the committee promised to make good on all lost back pay after just two quarters of profitability, believing thereby that morale would be sustained. But Judith warned that what was seen as a wise fiscal move by the decision-makers was going to be experienced as a breach of trust with those who meanwhile had to rely on family and friends to make their house payments.

Rationalization

When the first manager was caught with fraudulent expenses on his report, Judith was disappointed but not surprised. She knew that once trust had been breached, vulnerable individuals would find ways to justify all manner of ethical lapses. *I was just collecting what I was rightfully owed. I worked late every day last week. This makes up for the receipts for my bridge tolls I forgot to turn in three years ago.* Unfortunately, Judith's prediction had proven true. As the days rolled by, rationalizations were becoming more and more elaborate until, one day, she heard the excuse whose predictable arrival she had most dreaded: *Everybody does it.*

Managing up, Judith took each infraction as a cue to raise her level of protest to the entrenched committee: *Let's find another way to make up the shortfall. This way is too costly for us.* Managing down, she told her employees that she would do everything she could within her power to get the policy changed but *meanwhile, this is it.*

Act Three: Some time down the road, TWA finally had two profitable quarters in a row. Back pay was duly restituted but by then, the damage to morale had been done.

What happened at TWA illustrates the mechanism by which corporate cultures gradually degrade from an ethical team working toward a unified goal to an ethic of each one for him or herself. If the rank and file believe that their trust has been breached—you can fire as many transgressors as can figure out clever ways to pad an expense account, steal company supplies, take bribes and so on and on—others will come up from behind to take their place. Their crimes will be subtler and their rationalizations more elaborate. Until root causes are addressed, ethical lapses will continue to make curtain calls, even though nobody will be applauding.

Discovery

Given the frequency with which variations of ethical issues present themselves over and over again in particular organizational contexts, you'd think that discovering root causes would be a difficult thing to do. It's not. Forget the fancy consultants. If you really want to know what's going on in your organization, just ask the hourly people, and you will hear more than you probably wished. The laundress in a hotel chain can explain to you exactly why a group of minimum wage employees started a little business on the side, selling filched comforters at flea markets. You will find yourself in a sophisticated conversation about the size of CEO compensation packages and the ratio between that of managers and of the rank and file. You can defend your hotel's payroll policies on the basis of utilitarian ethics— and you will obviously condemn stealing as morally wrong. But until the root issue is adequately addressed, you'd better double your order for replacement comforters.

Most of the time, having read just this much, you won't even need to leave your office to get at the root cause. Just ask yourself the simple question: *Is the ethical issue facing you or your organization a symptom or is it the root problem, itself? Are you working on the real problem?*

Figuring out the answer to this question is by and large something that leaders are capable of doing. So why don't we? It's not that root causes are difficult to unearth, after all. It's that we would rather not ask because if we understood the real issues afoot, we might have to do something about them. How badly do we really want to deal with the real stuff? Before we get back to why we *should* want to deal with root causes, let's examine all the pressures that conspire against us.

Pressures that conspire

Rationalization is not something that is done only by line workers when they are upset with management. Management is equally adept at rationalizing that they have sufficiently tackled an ethical issue when the truth is that they have addressed the problem only at the level they are willing to solve. Take the case of the pharmaceutical salesperson who is honored month after month for exponentially rising sales of a certain brand of painkiller. Then there comes the month that she is named in a government sting as a link in a drug abuse scheme by which certain pharmacies conspire to provide extraordinary amounts of the prescription medication to white collar addicts. She is fired. But the system of compensating salespeople for increased levels of sales that are clearly out of alignment with legitimate demand remains intact. The CEO goes public, wringing his hands, blaming the transgressions on the individual's flawed character. When a board member suggests that better procedures be put into place so that this never happens again, the executive committee convinces everybody that this was an isolated incident. To fix corporate policies would be time-consuming and laborious, and "if an individual wants to find a way to cheat, lie or steal, he or she will always find a loophole, anyway." So nothing is done, except handing out a new batch of awards to the next salespersons of the month.

It is true that most of us are in business to provide goods and/or services to our clients and customers. The more time we can spend doing so, the more we are likely to reap financial as well as other rewards. When we uncover bad news, we often encounter resistance in the organization. The entire system is oriented towards quick-fix solutions to mend the breach as quickly as possible, allowing us to return to our primary task: making and maximizing profits. This approach to dealing with ethical breaches is akin to a classic story taken from the Zen tradition. A respected elder in the community was taking a walk one evening when he came upon a woman on hands and knees, searching the dirt road for a gold coin she had lost. She had been there over an hour, going inch by inch over the area illuminated by the glow of a gas-lit lamp.

"An hour is a long time. Are you sure this is where you dropped the coin?" the elder inquired.

"Oh no," she answered. "I didn't lose it here. I lost it inside my house."

"Then why are you looking out here?"

"Because the light is better out here."

We tend only to admit to the things we will find easy to fix. This is why so often managers act first—then supply the appropriate reasons for their actions later. A well-known case history illustrates this point. Business ethics students routinely consider the time some decades ago that Carl Kotchian, the president of Lockheed Aircraft Corporation, struggled with a demand to pay representatives of Japanese government and business multi-million dollars in bribes and "commissions" in order to secure a huge deal to sell the L-1011 TriStar passenger jet to All Nippon Airlines. Lockheed was in financial peril, having failed to get some important contracts and losing others. Many of those who support Kotchian's position mount the argument that this was simply, if unfortunately, the way business was done in Japan, and that by going along, even if it was personally distasteful to him, Kotchian was providing people back home with much-needed work. Although a classroom full of aeronautical executives doing doctoral work in organizational leadership spent over an hour discussing the topic, nobody asked the question that should have been most obvious. Why was Lockheed in such a tenuous position in the first place that its very existence was on the line lest it compromise its values?

No big deal

It was a similar train of thought that transformed the space shuttle Columbia mission into a disaster. Engineers had incorrectly concluded that a mishap during liftoff posed no problem. It was, after all, just a small piece of foam, less than three pounds, that had broken off the external fuel tank, damaging the plates whose job it was to protect the craft from the intense temperatures encountered upon re-entry. If the scientists had followed common sense, and admitted that pieces of anything falling off a flying object going thousands of miles in space, subjected to something close to thousands of degrees of heat, could be problematical, they would have had to do something about it. They may have had to stall the space program; they may even have been reprimanded or replaced. Instead, they rationalized their doubts away and witnessed something much more disastrous than the delay of the launch or even the loss of a job: the unnecessary loss of lives. They'd gotten away with similar omissions before. Didn't anybody remember the O-ring that had failed in the Challenger disaster less than a decade prior?

And weren't *This is no big deal* and *Everybody does it*, by the way, the unspoken slogans of the 90s? When the stock market was booming, nobody seemed to care much if someone inside a company mentioned to family or friends that a stock price was about to rise or fall. The problems of insider trading, shady accounting practices, stock manipulation—all the unethical moves that suddenly seemed to be happening just after the turn of the century—had also laid down their roots in the dark.

The cost of ethics

So, here's a revolutionary notion: to run an ethical company, you've got to figure in the cost of being ethical. That means that sometimes doing business includes inconvenient delays, time-consuming corrections and investments in long-term solutions that will cost you some now, but will pay off later. In a later section, the chapter titled "The Ethical Organization," we will revisit this in greater depth, demonstrating through stories and statistics that the words "business ethics" are not self-canceling propositions.

But before we celebrate what is possible, let us revisit the Zen story one more time. If the story only involved one woman looking under the street lamp for what had been lost, that would be lesson enough. But in real life, the first person who comes along to witness her misguided search is not always a wise mentor, capable of waking her up with a probing question. In many workplaces, the first and second and third person who wanders by not only does not bother to shake her up—but willingly volunteers to join in the search where the light is brightest. In business, there's a name for these people: We call them "yes men"—people kept around by managers because they can be counted on to go along with the program.

Going with the flow is so engrained in many cultures, it often takes an outsider to state the obvious. Such was the case when Carol was hired as a consultant to write and lead the ritual scripts for the opening and closing ceremonies of a leading producer of fundraiser walks. One of the earlier walks, a cancer fundraiser in the south, was less than well received by walkers. After the event, managers were called together by the CEO who had sat out the event back at headquarters 3000 miles away. Everyone who had actually been there knew that trust with the walkers had been breached within the first hour, when march organizers neglected to mention to them that due to a last minute route change, the "starting line" was not where participants actually began their walk—but more than a mile down the road. The many walkers who had set time goals for themselves were behind before they'd even started. This disconnect was only compounded by additional permit problems that had forced the walkers onto unseasonably hot concrete sidewalks rather than the shaded walkways they'd expected, based on brochure pictures and descriptions promising ocean breezes and picturesque shorelines. In the midst of the sweltering crowd, the walk's regional manager whispered to Carol that she'd given early and repetitive notice to headquarters concerning both heat and permit issues, but the walk had gone on as scheduled.

Now the management team was gathered in the CEO's office to "discuss" what had gone wrong. "These walkers are wimps and whiners," the CEO announced. His solution: the demand that the inspirational tone of orientation scripts for upcoming walks be replaced by a scolding tone, meant to teach the women better manners. Carol suggested that perhaps the organization bore responsibility for producing a less than exemplary event. So shocked were the managers to hear someone question their leader, all remained silent—some literally turning their heads away and shielding their faces to distance themselves from the philistine. After a long, uncomfortable silence, the CEO's conversation concerning who was to be given the rewriting assignment proceeded, as if nothing had been said.

A fine line

The line between what is poor judgment and what is immoral can be a fine distinction, indeed. More often than not, we are dealing with somebody in power who is not so much deliberately unethical as who happens to have a personal agenda that is not particularly well thought through. In this case, the fact is that what was deemed ethical bore a striking similarly to that which put the leader in the best light and, by the way, required the least amount of soul-searching and self-correction. Such a combination of elements is at the very least a yellow flag on the play.

It was no surprise to many when the company lost its financial footing as a number of the events that had been on the books failed to attract the level of sign-ups needed to keep the company afloat. This was compounded by an increasing number of lawsuits stemming from a wide range of perceived transgressions. Running on a skeleton crew—primarily consisting of the people who had been silent in the room that fateful day—the company limped across the finish line with their handful of remaining events, laying off everybody else and shuttering the company's doors.

Good for whom?

Ethical lapses come about as the result of omissions and laziness perhaps even more frequently than conscious, intentional transgressions. But what causes omissions and laziness? Today's executives are increasingly faced with making numbers set by outside investors, pressured to cut costs and exceed expectations with diminishing human as well as material resources. Again, ethics requires an investment in not only energy, but time. If we are in cultures that often require us to move faster than the speed of thought—let alone conscience—we can understand how it is easier for all individuals in the chain of command who are being held accountable for results to gloss over indiscretions that in their personal lives, they simply would not tolerate.

Since we've pulled a classic Lockheed story from the treasure chest of ethics lore, let's pull out one—a more recent transgression—by Boeing. The story made headline news that someone in the Boeing sales force, a recent hire from Lockheed, had been using proprietary information from Lockheed to competitive advantage. An investigation concluded that Boeing had illegally obtained more than 25,000 Lockheed documents during initial bidding under the $2-billion program designed to launch seven U.S. military satellites into space. The individual was caught and Boeing was severely sanctioned by the Air Force—including the reassignment of the $560 million in contracts that Boeing had initially been awarded to Lockheed Martin. A global ethics meeting was called to reiterate to Boeing staff how important ethics is to the company.

Who is accountable?

But in situations such as this, how often is the real culprit held accountable? For instance, how often is the hiring manager who brought this salesperson on assigned a share in the responsibility? Perhaps he or she does not explicitly ask the salesperson to use confidential information on the company's behalf. But how far beneath the surface of the hiring manager's conscious thoughts was the possibility that something like this might somehow, perhaps inevitably, come about? When the salesperson comes back from meeting after meeting all aglow, how explicitly does the manager tune into his or her gut, paying attention to the growing suspicion that at least part of the success may be due to the inappropriate use of privileged information?

Mistakes were made

Perhaps our over-wrought corporate climate is the real root cause that needs to be addressed. But that does not relieve the individual of responsibility. Yes, individuals make mistakes; companies make mistakes. Some are intentional, some are inadvertent. Some people and companies get away with them, others get caught. There is a real issue, however, when leaders are so deeply out of touch that they don't even know that they've done or condoned something wrong.

Recruited as a CEO, Judith has on several occasions been offered the choice of whether and where to relocate the headquarters for the company she was to lead. Thinking of headquarters relocation as part of the package of perks, even the Board was surprised when she decided that moving the offices closer to her Los Angeles area home was not the best thing for the business. Chicago was the more appropriate choice. Judith had the insight that the company's headquarters had more to do with where the talent was, the geographical proximity to suppliers and airlines and so on, rather than her convenience. For many, this often is not the way it goes.

In the next section, we will turn our attention to an ethical decision-making process, designed to lead you step-by-step to resolution of specific issues in your workplace and life. The process will help you determine the best course of action to take, building rather than breaching trust, no matter what level of problem you choose to address. However, use it to get at root causes, and you will be among those who are changing the way we do business in our country and world. Short-term, you may find this developing ethical capability a terrible nuisance. Long-term, however, you will be providing ethical leadership of the highest caliber to your organization.

PART TWO

LEAP: The *Trust, Inc.* Decision-Making Process

Building Trust One Decision at a Time

Learn Everything You Can
Step One of LEAP

We come now to LEAP, the *Trust, Inc.* Decision-Making Process. LEAP is a practical, common sense approach to problem solving that makes an explicit connection between personal values and organizational goals. LEAP does not replace the structured problem solving methods you were taught in business school and leadership training programs. Judith is a great believer in the Total Quality Management approach, for example, having pioneered the notion of quality problem solving circles with great success in her division at FedEx. MBAs routinely study W. Edwards Deming, Philip B. Crosby and Peter Drucker, among others, and when they graduate into leadership positions, gain access to platoons of problem solving software programs and consultants. Each of their methods provides a helpful, structured approach to problem solving for today's complex business environments.

Nevertheless, daily headlines have made it increasingly apparent that organizational leaders can get themselves and their organizations into trouble when utilizing even the most respectable decision-making processes. The issue centers less around the quality of the problem solving technology, itself, and more on the motivation of the leader in charge and the nature of the environment in which he or she is operating. If the issue is perceived by both the individual and the organizational culture as one of political or economic efficacy versus doing the right thing, the battle for a quality solution is already lost.

For an illustration of how any method can be vulnerable to failure, take the case of brainstorming. There are many approaches to brainstorming, the most common being the free-form approach encouraging spontaneous suggestions, thoughts and ideas from anyone at the table. Virtually all of the brainstorming techniques call for a withholding of judgment by participants during the idea-generating phase. Whatever the method chosen, if the organizational culture is not a safe place in which to communicate candidly, people will consciously or unconsciously hold back their input. The self-censored suggestion that never makes it onto the table for fear of what others might secretly think could very well have been the very solution that would have delivered the sought-after results. In the LEAP process, there is no conflict between the operational solution and the ethical solution. They are, by definition, the same thing. Every step of the way, problems are viewed from the overarching perspective of how it is that we ought to lead. The best solutions, both operational and ethical, come about not despite our most deeply held values, but because of them.

LEAP One: Learning Everything You Can

With this in mind, we are now ready to begin with the first letter of the acronym LEAP, *L* for "Learn everything you can." You may recall the story of the CEO of the fundraiser production company who blamed the cancer walk's many problems on the state of mind of its whiny, unmotivated walkers. To maintain this position, he had to ignore early and repetitive notice to headquarters by the walk's regional manager concerning both weather and permit issues. The information to head this unfortunate situation off in advance was handily available to him. The real tragedy is that even when it was time to deal with the angry walkers after the fact, mend fences and put into place effective corrections for future walks, he was still unwilling to pay heed to the most readily available information sitting on his desk, already marked urgent.

When pausing to seek out, take in and seriously assess information that can potentially cause you personal discomfort and cost you time, energy and money, the quest for quality data can, in fact, not only take discipline but courage. Carol's public relations agency was faced with an ethical challenge that provides an apt illustration for this. They landed a rapidly growing chain of boutique hotels as a client. Their method was to take over architecturally interesting but dilapidated downtown buildings and transform them into trendy inns. For several years business boomed, a win/win situation for all concerned. But before long, others caught on to the trend and began opening competitive properties of their own.

One day, a meeting was called. It had been decided that the client's newest hotel would have an ancient Romanesque theme, prominently featuring in the lobby a rare and valuable antique fountain imported from France. The agency was invited to preview the fountain in order to describe it more eloquently to the media. Unfortunately, the account manager noticed one stray bit of information that had been meant to stay undiscovered. There was a price tag hanging from the back side, pronouncing it as, to excuse our French, "faux." The fountain was a two-month old fraud. The agency executive shared the information with her client, thinking that he had been duped. Instead, she was quietly told to forget about what she had seen.

When Carol's firm refused to go along with the lie, they were accused of disloyalty and criticized for not being good team players. Resigning was a simple—if painful—decision for them. The former client never did admit to his lie. Ethical lapses have a way of catching up with us, however. In this case, the reason the lie was told in the first place was that the company had been siphoning money from the marketing budget to pay top-heavy management salaries, most notably the CEO's own. As the competition in the marketplace heated up, the client had chosen to install the faux fountain in an effort to attract more attention from the press than a similarly priced but genuine fountain would have merited. Ironically, rather than allowing himself to be confronted by the black and white numbers on his own balance sheet, he lost his public relations agency at the exact moment he most needed their help. Before long, even elegant lies could no longer keep the facts at bay. He was forced to cut salaries across the board. Many of his managers jumped ship for operations that were run more ethically.

The pertinent information you may need to help you make the best decision is not always as simple a matter as reading a price tag inadvertently left to hang in full view. Situations with multiple stakeholders and points of view can challenge you with volumes of data, much of it contradictory. Which are the facts—which are bias, supposition or outright fabrication? You will have to make decisions about how to discern and retrieve the reliable information most pertinent to the situation at hand. Collect too little or the wrong kind of information, and you will be left behind where we were several chapters ago, making impulsive decisions on the basis of who can shout loudest across the ethical divide. The effort to do an exemplary job at data collection and analysis, however, can go equally awry. Gather too much and you can become hopelessly bogged down in detail.

Again, there are objective information gathering and structured assessment processes that can help you find the most efficient way to sort through the maze of possibilities. Professionally trained consultants are always ready to serve. The critical issue here is to note simply that the effectiveness of your decision will be based on the quality of the information you gather. It is worth the time and effort—and in many cases, the courage—to go after the best data available or, in some cases, to pay attention to the information already in hand. On this foundation, you will put yourself in the optimum position for generating options that address the real issues.

Defining the problem

Whatever information gathering method you use, defining the nature of the issue with which you are faced is the critical first step toward learning everything you can. As we suggested in the last chapter on root causes, you can't solve the wrong problem and get the resolution you seek. Before we show you how to use the information you gather to shovel down to the root of the issue, we suggest that it is just as important to know where to dig. Dr. Edward de Bono built his career teaching his classic thinking course to students at prestigious universities around the world, from Harvard to Cambridge. One of his most enduring bits of wisdom is also his simplest. In his classic *de Bono's Course in Thinking*, we are taught how to reduce an otherwise unruly problem to manageable size. In virtually every conflict, de Bono argues, there are already areas of agreement between individuals and groups on all sides of an issue. These overlapping areas, be they facts, values or points of view, are not the problem. Acknowledge them and set them aside. Next, recognize that there are issues that at first glance may seem worthy of attention but are, in fact, irrelevant. Set these aside, as well. After the areas of agreement and irrelevance are subtracted, what remains is the core of the conflict—the real crux of the problem to be solved.

In the example of the fake fountain, the nature of the ethical issue was close to the surface. Not all issues are so clearly delineated. For instance, ethical issues do not come about only as the result of conflict. Ethical concerns may also address issues in the organization that need improvement, anticipating problems before they arise. Judith, then serving as vice president of her group at FedEx, noted the number of worker's comp claims filed by couriers that were coming across her desk. Her group's safety statistics were already among the best across the divisions. Some would argue, therefore, that this was not an ethical issue in the first place and that good enough is just that: enough. However, it was Judith's conviction that if accidents could be avoided, it was impingent upon management to look for and address the cause. Judith's first impulse was to seek out the opinions of people on the front lines who actually do the job, in this case, the couriers themselves. These are the very people that managers often exclude, on the basis that they don't have the "right" to be there. In the spirit of learning everything you can, however, Judith not only did not fear what she might hear, but welcomed the input. She quickly called management and couriers together into a quality roundtable to brainstorm solutions.

Once assembled, Judith's method was simple and effective: "I ask 'Why?' a lot." As it turned out, a number of the accidents were related to the couriers slipping on the floor in the loading area. But why was this happening? The floor was no different than others that received just as much foot traffic. Then one of the couriers offered that the floor gets slippery when wet. All the floors got slippery when wet, and they weren't a cause for concern. Why was this particular floor different? Because this wasn't just a case of washing and mopping the floor on a routine basis. This floor became wet and slippery every time it rained, the water splashing in with the arriving and departing trucks. Given the tight schedules couriers kept, there was seldom time to mop the floor. That was the exact location and circumstances during which the accidents occurred. The root of the problem had been uncovered. Now what to do about it? The group threw out a wide range of suggestions for consideration.

Once a list of possibilities had been generated, questions continued to drive the problem solving process. Taking the best suggestions back to her management team, Judith's quest for information took on a different tone. *What are the advantages and disadvantages of the various suggestions? Which factors should be given the most weight? What are the cost-benefit ratios? The probabilities and feasibilities?* The best suggestion to come out of this structured process was to put a new coating on the floor in the rain-prone area that would not become slippery when wet. This was not the cheapest of the alternatives. In fact, where short-term economic prudence could well have been justified in terms of just letting it go, Judith chose to put employee welfare first. The operational and ethical solutions were the same. Subsequently, not only were worker's comp claims down, but morale among couriers was raised. Moreover, Judith's timely investment may well have paid off many times over when compared with the potential for expensive lawsuits and fines related to worker's injuries on the job. The process had delivered such a positive result that the concept was soon taken region-wide in FedEx.

What is the pertinent information?

As is demonstrated by the case of the slippery floor, gathering information can often illuminate that which is the right thing to do. On the most basic level, there are the obvious questions that need to be addressed. What does the law have to say about this situation? What is company policy? Is there a professional code that may be violated? If solving your problem were simply a matter of clarifying what the compliance ramifications could be to you or to your organization, your fact-finding quest has come to an end. You have discovered everything you need to know to make the right decision. Ignore what you have found at your own peril.

Even in the case of complex issues, better information—or at least a less biased appraisal of the facts in hand—can often make one path or another the obvious way to go. But not always. In our earlier discussion of the Golden Rule, we spoke of times when the ethical core of the issue is not clearly defined by right versus wrong, but right versus right. Equally daunting: there are situations where there seems to be no right at all. Every obvious decision bears a cost for someone— or everyone. Now you find yourself face-to-face with multiple points of view and agendas.

Who are the stakeholders and what can you learn from them?

One of your first responsibilities as an ethical leader facing a multi-faceted ethical issue is to decide who should be invited into the conversation. These interested parties are the stakeholders: individuals who bear responsibility for influencing or making an ethical decision on a particular issue as well as those who may hold neither rights nor power in regard to the decision that will be made, but who will be impacted by the consequences. Some of the players will be obvious. Some less so. However, if you look around the table and you are only surrounded by conversation partners who agree with you—beware! You cannot make a quality decision without access to the information and input of all those who have a stake in your decision, especially those with whom you may disagree.

In the best-case scenario, you already know who these players are and you have been in communication with them on a regular basis. When Judith had the responsibility of expanding FedEx into 17 states and Canada, she knew that there was the potential for problems with local communities who could question everything from the location of distribution centers in suburban neighborhoods to the increasing number of noisy airplanes flying overhead. So early in its history that the company was known less as FedEx and more as "Fed Who?" Judith sent the sales force door-to-door, meeting the stakeholders before they even knew that they constituted an interested party. The goal was to reassure the community that FedEx would be a good neighbor, welcoming their input and involvement in the earliest stages.

Can we agree on the facts?

At the information gathering stage of ethical decision-making, the immediate goal is not to convince others that your take on the situation is right. Rather, the task at hand is to sort through heaps of unprocessed data with the intention of defining a common body of facts upon which all the interested parties can mutually agree. Here's a useful approach. Put all the data you've gathered on the table, including the alternatives, arguments and information supplied by the stakeholders on this issue. Then, take away the biases, opinions, prejudices, assumptions, preferences and the like. What remains will be the facts. Remove subjectivity and you go a long way towards eliminating the sources and causes of unreliable and misleading information, as well. Or, as Judith is fond of telling both employees and negotiating partners: You may be entitled to your own opinions, but not to your own facts. Here's a checklist to guide you through this challenging task.

THE OBJECTIVITY CHECKLIST

- **Bias:** *The particular lens of values and beliefs through which you view issues and make judgments about them.* Your values and beliefs are important and can return at a later date to play an appropriate role. But at this early, critical juncture, it is important to recognize that there is a difference between your own personal biases and the biases of others—as well as what constitutes objective fact. Prejudice is an extreme form of bias and is best disposed of as quickly and thoroughly as possible.

- **Opinion:** *The conclusion you have come to concerning the issue at hand.* Again, this represents your own personal belief based on what seems to you to be true. As with bias, however, opinion concerns itself primarily with what ought to be done and less with what is objectively true. Beware, particularly, of opinions formulated before or while fact gathering is still in progress.

- **Assumption:** *The position that takes for granted that your biases and opinions are objective truth that should be shared by all.* Unfortunately, others have their own differing sets of assumptions and/or its close cousin, conjecture. None of these are, in and of themselves, to be confused with objective fact.

- **Preferences:** *The prescription for what you feel, think and/or believe should be done.* Your preferences may be powerful. They should at some point even be seriously taken into consideration in the form of a proposal. But know this: they may or may not be based on fact. If they are not, these, too, should be set aside.

Assuming you've successfully sorted out the subjectivity to make possible a more objective consideration of the situation, the state of the facts remaining becomes obvious. In the optimal scenario, the facts are now empowered to speak for themselves and everyone aligns themselves around what have clearly emerged as the facts of the matter. But it is possible, too, that precious little has survived the strategic sorting process. Perhaps the only fact that remains is that you may never be able to gather enough data to make the decision with which you are faced a simple one. While there will be important things about the situation that you don't know you are capable of discovering, sometimes there will be things you'd dearly like to put your hands on that can never be known. We cannot know the future, for instance. We cannot control or anticipate every possible factor or outcome. At some point, you will have researched, mulled and discussed enough. At that juncture, the ethical leader recognizes that his or her quest for sufficient data to make a risk-free decision may have become an excuse not to act at all. When you can no longer, in good conscience, put off making a decision, often your only refuge is to take comfort in the fact that even if neither your process nor your results are perfect, at the very least, a better decision than would otherwise have come about, can still be made.

What if we agree on the facts but still can't come to consensus on what to do?

Sometimes, even after making the attempt to strip away subjectivity, there remains profound and resistant disagreement between positions. While your situation is difficult, it is not hopeless. There is at least one final fact upon which you can agree—namely, that the crux of your problem is rooted not in the realm of data and facts, but at the level of values and beliefs. In Marvin T. Brown's *The Ethical Process*, the author makes this critical point, suggesting that now the discourse becomes not about numbers, ratios and costs but rather about the evaluation of divergent assumptions regarding how the world ought to be.

Brown notes that there are three levels of values and beliefs with which we may need to deal: the organizational, the social and the individual. At the organizational level, each of the stakeholders ponders what the stand they take will say about the kind of organization they believe themselves to be leading. At the social level, the key question becomes, "What is our responsibility in relation to the kind of society in which we want to live?" At the individual level, we consider the ramifications of our decision in terms of how we see ourselves as human beings—and where we draw the line between what is acceptable and what is not for us personally.

For ethical leaders, even if arrived at as the last resort, confronting head-on and engaging in genuine discourse about the things that really matter is not experienced as a failure but rather as a relief. Once you begin, you find yourself newly empowered to pierce through the cloudiness that can obscure access to the authentic depths where genuine problem solving can transpire. You do not get to pick the nature of the ethical dilemma that is yours to solve. Some issues are at the surface, easy to resolve. Others will take you deeper than you'd expected you'd ever have to go, changing you, your organization and even the society within which you live profoundly, in ways you had not previously anticipated.

Evaluate Your Options
Step Two of LEAP

In step one of the *Trust, Inc.* Decision-Making Process, we addressed the importance of learning everything you can about the dilemma with which you are faced. For starters, you reduced the situation to manageable size by setting aside areas that are either already in agreement or beside the point to expose the core of the conflict that yet needs to be addressed. You then sought out facts and data to provide you with added perspective. Some of the information was relatively easy to unearth: What does the law have to say about this situation? Company policy? If there's been time, you've opened up meaningful dialogue with individuals likely to be impacted, building bridges of trust. When there hasn't been, you've done your best to give serious, objective consideration to all the voices—internal and external—that have a stake in the outcome. Above all, you've learned the importance of questioning the reliability of your sources and your interpretations.

It is possible that, by now, you've already come up with the solution to your problem. If it were simply a matter of clarifying what is in accordance with the law or company policy, for instance, of course now that you know, you will make the decision that complies with the rules. Perhaps, too, you have already discovered that better information—or a less biased appraisal of the facts in hand—has made one path or another the obvious choice. If so, your decision-making process—this time around—is over. Now it is time to act.

But what about those times when you peel away conjecture, bias and supposition only to reveal that compelling arguments pro and con remain, demanding to be reconciled? What about conflicting loyalties or rights, all of which can make valid claims? What about clashing value systems, each supported by fully realized communities and justifications? What about your own inner conflicts—those times you struggle against your fear about whether the decision you come to will build or breach trust? And finally, what about those times when your boss or board challenges your conclusion, leaving you shaken or confused? Inevitably, there will be those times when you find that living up to your own standards of holding yourself accountable may exact a bigger price than you wish you had to pay.

When facts aren't enough

Step two assumes that you've done your homework, but that rather than feeling empowered by the knowledge you've accumulated, you are feeling humbled. The truth is that as much information as you've already gathered, as long as there is a decision yet to be made, there are more questions to be answered. The disturbing news is that there may never be enough facts to make the decision with which you are faced a simple one. In fact, it is likely that the more information you gather—and the more honest the lens through which you view it—the harder your decision may be.

In our age of technological advances, for instance, you may discover that there are quite simply no reliable precedents upon which to draw. The healthcare industry is faced daily with new procedures that prolong life, the broader implications of which have yet to be explored. But ethical issues relating to health and the public good can be found in many industries. Take the food business, for example. We can test and test again until the cows literally come home—but what can this tell us about what eating genetically altered steak may be doing to generations to come? We have previously emphasized the importance of separating fact from conjecture. But how does one project without conjecture the future impact of cloning, organ implants, new pesticides, and the like? This is not just a question of keeping faith with the future for the CEO of the world's largest food manufacturer, by the way. This is also a question for the general manager of the local supermarket, who must make the decision whether or not to stock the new and "improved" items for sale to his or her customers. And, too, this is a question for the employee of the international chain that expects him or her to carry out the decision without dissent.

Not every complex issue that holds the potential to build or breach trust is something for the science fiction books. What about everyday ethical dilemmas that are situated not simply in the black and white territory of right and wrong—but in the gray? Take, for instance, conflicts between customer service and product quality. What if your company's future depends upon your delivering a minor component for electric shavers to a key customer on time—but you have just become aware of a manufacturing error that might cause the product to fail years down the road. Even though the breakdown will occur long after the warranty will have expired, are you obligated to inform the customer? And even if you know this would be a good thing to do, what is your responsibility to your company? Do you risk losing your biggest customer and putting your company's future at risk for something that may or may not happen somewhere down the road? Then, too, there is the issue of conflicting values, rights and definitions of fairness in an increasingly global marketplace. In one country, bribery can be considered to be a legitimate way of doing business—a way of acknowledging the contributions individuals in positions of power have made towards fulfilling business partners' goals. In another, bribery can be seen as the abuse of power, bringing harm to the majority for the advantage of one. As we explored in chapter two, the Golden Rule can go a long way towards helping us to build trust on common ground—but it cannot fill in every one of our increasingly diverse religious, spiritual and cultural gaps.

Again, it is sometimes possible that the more you know, the less likely mutual resolution appears to be an achievable goal. When agreement is not even conceivably possible, all that remains is 1) compromise on one or everybody's part, or 2) a daring decision to hold one's moral ground and take the consequences, whatever they may be.

Decision-making as risk

We like to think that we can use rational processes to come up with the most ethical solution for all concerned. In fact, Aristotle was but the first in a long line of philosophers who suggested that the use of one's intellect gives human beings the best shot at a virtuous life. Many of the processes that are commonly taught in business schools are based on the hopeful notion that logic can unlock the puzzle of whatever challenges come our way. To make this work, most decision-making processes hypothesize idealized scenarios featuring reasonable actors and contexts.

In real life, people often react emotionally, inconsistently, irrationally, politically—or a combination of all four and more—especially when faced with a dilemma that has the potential to make or break one's reputation. In any given conference room, venting, denial and rationalization may all be going on simultaneously—sometimes in the very same person. On the street outside, wafting in through plate glass windows, equally real demonstrators are waving signs and shouting epithets. As we have addressed previously, even with the best of intentions and preparation, your decision-making theory—if you even have one—may shift, detour or fail when faced with real life challenges. You may discover that no matter how many levels of bias you peel away, there are yet more to go. And these are the best among us, who are at least making the attempt to struggle with complex issues—not to mention our own human natures—with not enough time, too much pressure and a whole lot at stake.

Because you are taking the time to read this book, you are way ahead of the game. Aristotle, et al., were right to the extent that thinking about things is at the very least better than not thinking about things. But the truth is that decision-making always carries an element of risk. In fact, what is needed is not a decision-making tool that will lead to the perfect solution—but one that acknowledges and reduces the element of risk as much as possible in order to create the likeliest environment in which to come up with a better solution than would otherwise have come about. You cannot assume that everyone who has a stake in the issues will like your decision. But you can do everything possible to stay true to the values that are the building blocks of trust: honesty, consistency, clarity and fairness. The process we are about to share with you makes no promises that decision-making will be easy—only that you will have a decision-making tool providing you with the most reliable and meaningful means by which to address the complexities.

A leap of faith

That said, before we begin sharing the specifics of step two of the *Trust, Inc.* Decision-Making Process with you, we are going to take a leap of faith. The leap we are taking is this: that you do, indeed, value trust. With all the variables we've addressed to date—encouraging you to question just about everything you've been taught about judging right and wrong in the past—you may be surprised to hear that we believe that there is something you can count on in the decision-making process. Not only do we propose that your desire to build rather than breach trust can serve as the enduring touchstone in the process, we contend that without this core motivation, your attempts to resolve complex issues will be flawed.

As we discussed in chapter two, the reason that your core values are even more important than your ethical theory is because they form the lens through which theory will inevitably be viewed. If you are a utilitarian, you will define and value happiness, for example, according to your own definition. If you are a Kantian rights or duties ethicist, you will select which rights or duties take precedence based on your own conception. The truth is, supposedly objective ethical theory can be manipulated, consciously or unconsciously, to serve your own ends. This can be a good thing if your values are in keeping with humanity's highest aspirations directed toward serving the greater good. Or it could be a bad thing, if one is so mired in temptation, greed or expediency that rationalization is mistaken for truth. In other words, any ethical decision-making process only works to the degree that it is being used by ethical people. To be an ethical person means that you have done the hard work of bringing to consciousness your own core values: your deeply held sense of how things ought to be, and your conviction that how things ought to be is good. Not only have you become aware of what you inwardly deem to be important, but you have allowed yourself to be tested.

Recalling the name exercise you did in chapter two, take a moment now to think of the ten or more most important qualities and characteristics that give your life meaning. Keeping each value to as succinct a description as possible, such as "trust," "honesty," "love," "health" and so on, write each value down on a separate index card. Now, organize the cards in order of importance to you. To help you find your number one value, pick any of the cards at random and pose the following question to yourself: *Could any of the other qualities in the deck be possible if this quality didn't exist?*

For instance, health and self-respect may be two of your top qualities. If you have chosen the quality of "health" at random from your deck, you now look at "self-respect" by asking: *Even if I weren't healthy, could I still respect myself?* If the answer is yes, self-respect now goes to the top of the deck. Continue with this exercise until your stack of core values is in order. Please note that it is possible that the placement of your values may change over time. For instance, take the values of health and job security. A young person in good health might reasonably ask the question: *Even if I didn't have job security, could I still be healthy?* In this case, the answer might well be yes. You would put health above job security in your stack of values. However, there may come a time when you or someone for whom you care develops a condition requiring on-going medical attention. Now, the answer to the question may be *no—you (or your dependent) cannot be healthy without the benefit of job security.* You might be in a situation where staying in a particular job for the health insurance, alone, is, in truth, a matter of life and death. What ends up on our lists, as well as their order of ranking, reflects not only the particular influences that formed us but the unique life circumstances that continue to shape our values as long as we are alive. In other words, your list will be uniquely yours, appropriate to you at this point in your life. When you have your core values organized, set the deck nearby for reference later in this chapter.

A best practices decision-making process

We are ready now to embark on the second letter of the acronym LEAP: Evaluate Your Options. Having invited you to join us in a leap of faith into deeper dimensions, this step is particularly helpful in our complex times. Processes consulted in its development include the Potter Box by Ralph Potter of Harvard University, Laura L. Nash's classic 12-question process, as first shared in "Ethics Without the Sermon," *Harvard Business Review*, as well as suggested approaches by the Public Relations Society of America. Our best practices process assumes that you may be operating in less than ideal circumstances and that logic, alone, can only go so far. As a value-added feature, step two can be used to address any level of problem. If you are under extreme pressure and need a quick fix, you will find this an expedient and productive decision-making tool. After you've handled the emergency, you will be given the tools to seek longer-term solutions addressing root causes.

Step Two: Evaluate Your Options

In the last chapter, you defined and clarified the problem facing you. Now it is time to generate and evaluate possible solutions that will support your efforts to build relationships of mutual trust within your organization as well as with your various stakeholders. Answer each area of inquiry in order. Some of the questions are meant to be worked through on your own, writing down your responses as you go. Others will benefit from conversation with others, either one-on-one or in a group setting. Here are the seven areas of inquiry.

1. What outcome do you want?

It is no accident that this, the first question, is also a loaded one. Right from the start, you are asked to be scrupulously honest with yourself. Of course, there is the simplest level of response, having to do with the outcome you hope to realize through your decision. Chances are your first answer will be something along the lines that you want the problem resolved so that the greatest good accrues to all concerned—including, of course, your own best interests. Even on this first pass answer, however, take the time to be as specific as possible. Who are the players you hope to satisfy? What would it look like if the problem were resolved? What kind of impact would a successful outcome have on your career, your organization, you community?

Then, there are the even more challenging considerations. For instance, are you looking for a quick-fix solution—the moral minimum that will stamp out this fire and allow you to get back to work as quickly as possible? Or do you hope to achieve longer-term resolution, knowing that unless you are willing to dig deep to address the root causes, whatever went wrong in the first place is likely to go wrong again? What level of this problem are you attempting to solve?

2. What makes this an issue of trust?

Quite simply, the situation with which you are faced is a matter of trust if there are values such as honesty, consistency, fairness and courage at risk...yours, your organization's and/or any of the stakeholders who have an interest in the outcome. This is why we asked you to write down your core values ahead of time and keep them by your side. Survey your deck. What are the specific values that are at risk? How high up are these particular values in your deck? The higher up the value, the less you will want to make compromises you will regret. Perhaps, too, you may realize that your deck of values needs refinement. For instance, loyalty may be high on everybody's list of values. But the real issue may well be loyalty to whom? You may be torn between loyalty to your company and loyalty to the community. In fact, if one of your core value cards reads simply "loyalty," you may find that you have to edit it to read more specifically one way or the other, or add another card to your stack. You can change your deck at will. Just make sure that when you rearrange, rewrite, add or subtract a card, it is clarification and not rationalization that is moving your pen.

3. What options haven't you thought of yet that could satisfy all the stakeholders in this issue? If you think of a satisfying solution at this juncture, you are done.

If you have done your homework, your subconscious mind has already been busy at work processing all the information you've gathered. Now is an opportune moment to generate possible solutions. Forget about all your prior attempts to reason things through. This is the perfect time for creative brainstorming. Whether you are working on your own or in a group, refrain from censoring any of the ideas that are thrown out. Approach this challenge with an air of expectancy, assuming that a breakthrough is possible. If after a reasonable period of time you still have not come up with an acceptable solution, it's time for even more radical measures. Read on.

4. If you were willing to compromise your own or your organization's values, what would a possible solution look like? What would the cost be to you? To your organization? To other stakeholders?

Chances are that if you haven't come up with a suitable solution thus far, it is because nobody has been willing to budge on aspects that they consider to be critical—or that you, personally, are mired in ambivalence. If you are stuck, try shock therapy. Put forward your best, most convincing argument and then argue effectively against it. How does the problem look from an adversarial point of view? What solution might a challenger propose? Could you live with their solution, or some reasonable variation? If not, why not? Where do you draw the line between trade-offs, compromising or selling out? If you find yourself unwilling to bend, breach or trash your values for expediency's sake, read on.

5. If you are unwilling to compromise your own values, what could the ramifications to you be? To your organization? To all the other stakeholders?

Suppose you have a hunch you know what you should do. What is keeping you from acting on it? Perhaps you recognize that there is a cost to acting out of your principles that you would rather not have to pay. Are your concerns realistic? It is possible that you need to seek support from someone in a position of power, assuring you that you will not suffer for doing the right thing? If you cannot get such an assurance, what will it cost you to act on principle? Is this a cost you are willing to bear? Do you have an alternative you can live with?

6. Do any of your solutions thus far satisfy your answer to question one: What are you hoping to achieve?

Take the best solution you've arrived at thus far and test it against your answer to question one. In particular, ask yourself:

- Does your solution address to your satisfaction the players you've identified as having a stake in the outcome of your decision?
- Does your solution achieve longer-term resolution, addressing root causes, or were you willing to settle for a quick-fix solution even knowing that what went wrong in the first place is likely to go wrong again?
- Does your solution coincide with your values? Is it more likely to build or breach trust?
- Is what you are thinking you will do the same as what you should do?
- Are you being honest with yourself?

7. What remains to be resolved?

If you are fortunate, your answer to this question may well be *nothing*. If, for instance, what you will do matches what you should do—and both respond to your original intention—your issue is resolved. Now all that is left is to implement your decision.

But what if you've reached this stage of the process and even your best attempt comes up short? You know you are confused, dissatisfied or frustrated. Or perhaps you are convinced that you have found the only possible solution—but the pit of your stomach is telling you otherwise. Have you misinterpreted the data? Could circumstances change? What if your decision was somehow made public? Could this backfire on you somehow?

The good news is that we are only halfway through the *Trust, Inc.* decision-making process, with two more steps to go. At this juncture, it is progress enough to refuse to settle for a slick or superficial resolution. Now you are ready for step three: Access Intuition, where you will find yourself capable and willing to make the decision that you can count on to build rather than breach trust.

Access Your Intuition
Step Three of LEAP

Most problem solving processes begin and end with deductive reasoning, which is also the primary mode that we've been in during the first two steps of LEAP as well: 1) **L**earn everything you can about the situation; 2) **E**valuate your options in order to make the most logical decision, compatible with your values and aspirations. Deductive decision-making models suffer, however, in the same way that weather forecasting models fall short of predicting climate particulars accurately for more than a few days out. Even with the help of supercomputers and irrefutable laws of physics, neither has proven able to hold its own under the weight of all the variables. It is as true of a cloud as it is of the whim of an individual.

When it comes to ethical decision-making, logic is only half the story. Human beings are complex, with emotional and spiritual as well as intellectual and physical needs. During this, the third step of LEAP, you will be guided to use not just your logic but your intuition, tapping into the whole, wider spectrum of your cognitive capabilities to address the problem at hand. If you think you already have a solution to the ethical challenge you are facing, you will use this step as a fail-safe test, making sure that the option you have chosen not only fits the criteria of rational coherency—but passes muster with the most important judge of all: your gut. If you don't yet have an answer that meets your expectations, accessing your intuition could well deliver the breakthrough that previously eluded you.

The limits of logic

De Bono, the professor of thinking skills and strategies, shares a favorite anecdote illustrating the limits of logic. The story centers on the city of London. Some years ago, the city made a major investment in an advanced computer system to weigh multiple variables to determine the location of the area's third airport. The data, including the needs, concerns and interests of the various stakeholders, environmental factors and regulations went into the computer and the ideal location came out. As soon as the "best" location was announced, public outcry drowned out the experts' findings. Common sense prevailed with a more suitable site selected. The problem: the computer programmers had failed to anticipate public objection to the noise level of the flight paths of jets as they flew over neighborhoods.

Of course, the first question to be asked in hindsight was whether the leadership team had actually gone into the neighborhood eliciting the community's concerns. This was a major point in step one of LEAP which cited the experience of reaching out to neighbors one-by-one when opening new markets for FedEx. Whether or not the London airport leadership team solicited community input, it could still have been possible in the massive gathering of data to have inadvertently left something out. But then the question becomes: was there no one involved in the airport leadership who did not have some kind of uneasy feeling in the pit of his or her stomach—some premonition—that something was amiss? It is not only possible but imperative for logic and intuition to work hand-in-hand.

Intuition defined

What is intuition? Hunter Lewis, in his book, *A Question of Values*, identifies intuition as "a highly developed and powerful mode of purely abstract mental processing, one that synthesizes masses of facts and theories with extraordinary speed." This understanding of intuition is supported by John Beebe's discussion in his book *Integrity in Depth*. "Intuition brings us a sense of the ecology of integrity, for intuition is the function that gives a feeling for the entire pattern operating in a given moment." Intuition, by our definition, is the innate human capacity to synthesize massive quantities of data to arrive at seemingly spontaneous solutions beyond that which logical processes alone would have deduced.

The Greek mathematician Archimedes experienced intuition when, having exhausted himself trying to work out the principle of specific gravity, he gave himself a break by taking a bath. As he stepped into the tub, he noticed that the water level rose. This experiential clue provided the breakthrough solution he had been seeking. As the story goes, he shot out of the bath and ran stark naked down the streets of ancient Greece shouting, "Eureka!" Centuries later Carl Jung, confused and upset about his break with his mentor Sigmund Freud, had a similar breakthrough. Having retreated to his family home to lick his wounds, he found himself on the floor playing children's games. Soon he took his childhood fantasies out into the backyard, and built out of stone the villages, towns, and forts he'd imagined as a young boy. Spontaneously, he was overtaken by the realizations that form the basis of Jungian psychology.

In many companies, individuals who are caught "day-dreaming" at their desks would be judged as not working. We, however, recognize the possibility for a different interpretation. As a popular story from the Zen tradition tells us, a certain disciple crossed many miles to study with an important teacher. When he arrived, he tried to impress the master with how hard he had worked and studied to get to this day. Coolly, the master invited him to tea. The more the disciple talked, the more tea the master poured. Before long, the tea had spilled out over his cup, onto his lap and the floor. "Master! What are you doing?" the disciple cried out. "You are like this teacup, the master explained." You are so full, there is no room for anything new to come into you. Come to me with your teacup empty, and then we may begin." This is not only a matter of eastern philosophy, by the way. John Adams, one of the founders of our country, said something along these lines when he advised his fellows: "The mind must be loose."

The value of instinct

Running a variety of sizes, styles and types of businesses, both of us routinely pay heed to our gut instincts as a way to supplement and illuminate the rational problem-solving methods we are utilizing, each step of the way. When co-leading what was then one of the largest independent public relations agencies in the country, Carol made national news with her concept of inner excellence: the creation of a business environment that built time into the workday to mull and reflect without guilt or subterfuge. We are not alone, as many organizational leaders have learned to value receiving as well as pushing as a means of mental processing, allowing for new ideas and insights to emerge spontaneously into consciousness. It takes time and space, after all, to ponder the implications of one's actions and decisions, to project into the future, to reflect on deeper issues of meaning and to access creativity. Among those sold on the concept of making time for intuition were half a dozen federal employees who regularly gathered for time to reflect silently in a quiet conference room. Where? The Pentagon. Another correspondent, a manager in Portland, Oregon, told us that when he observes himself to be spinning his wheels, he puts his work down and does a crossword puzzle. Central to the Apple Computer legacy is the story about former CEO John Sculley who shocked the computer industry by taking off for his ranch in Maine not long after taking the reins of the company. There, he put aside the overwhelming problems that had greeted his arrival. While designing a barn for the property he had a spontaneous breakthrough, returning with plans to streamline management. Following his return, he quadrupled Apple's revenues to more than $4 billion.

Metaphorically, intuition is like water filling up behind the wall of a dam. As we go through our lives, our subconscious minds are constantly gathering data, learning from experiences, generating ideas and making connections. From the other side of the dam, it can look like absolutely nothing is happening. Then, one last drop causes the pooling water to pour over the top in the form of insight and creativity. For many people, the intuitive breakthrough process we share later in this chapter constitutes that one final drop. But you don't need a formal process to access your intuition.

The lost keys

We all have the capacity to solve problems by accessing our intuition, receiving and letting, as well as by making and doing. Here is an example that will undoubtedly be familiar to you. Have you ever misplaced your keys? If you are like most of us, chances are your first impulse was to approach the problem logically. *Where did I see my keys last? Were they in the pocket of the last coat I was wearing? In which room did I last see them?* And so on. This approach works most of the time. You find your keys. However, have you ever gone through every one of your logical problem-solving techniques, and still not known where the keys are? What do you do then? At some point, most of us temporarily set the issue aside and place our thoughts elsewhere. We answer the phone, get some coffee, whatever. And what happens? *The location of the keys pops into your mind.* Did you make that knowledge appear? Of course not. What you did do was spontaneously create an environment in which your inner knowing could reveal the location of your keys to your conscious mind.

Most of us are so busy wrestling our linear processes to the ground in the effort to force out a solution, we do not provide a space for ourselves or others for insights to break through to us spontaneously. As the lost key example demonstrates, your intuition is working beneath the surface of your everyday thoughts every moment of your life. In point of fact, while your normal, routine mind has been busily working to solve the ethical problem facing you, your subconscious mind has also been faithfully gathering new evidence, data, experiences, and ideas just ready to break through. Again, you cannot make this kind of knowing happen for you. But you can learn to create the environment in which this kind of knowing is most likely to take place. Too, you can train yourself to pay attention to the insights that do arise, learning that when you come to trust yourself, you can also come to trust your intuition. This step of LEAP suggests that if you can create an environment for something as common as the location of your lost keys to pop into your mind, might it not be possible to use this process to intuit the solutions to your bigger problems as well?

A message from the past

For Judith, one such experience occurred following 9/11. At the time, Judith was serving as CEO of La Petite Academy, a multi-million dollar company providing daycare services for over 80,000 preschoolers at both independent and corporate sites. The management team had been in the midst of a branding campaign, seeking points of differentiation from the competition. Feeling that the sessions were understandably unproductive, Judith took a rare time out from her duties, taking a longer walk than usual. As she walked, doing nothing more than watching the wind in the trees, a memory suddenly popped into her mind. She remembered that when she was a young girl—not even 12 years of age—she'd taken a similar walk, longer than usual, on her way home from school. That time it had been in Chicago, the urban terrain of her childhood. At the time, the young Judith had been mulling over the fact that more and more of her friends' parents, the mothers as well as the fathers, were taking full-time jobs. Suddenly, the thought occurred to her that parents would increasingly be depending on the schools to teach future generations the Golden Rule and other important values.

Years later, now the CEO of a multi-million dollar company, Judith spontaneously realized that this unbidden memory from deep in her past was bearing with it a message worth heeding. Parents did, indeed, need the schools to help fill in the gaps while they were at work. La Petite could do both the right thing in terms of creating meaning in a post-9/11 world and fulfill the company's obligation to market effectively, by incorporating a values and character development program into the educational curriculum, something both concerned parents and corporations would like. The program, called Kids of Character, was subsequently introduced to the La Petite Academy community, meeting great response.

A word of caution

Shortly, you will be given the nuts and bolts of step three of LEAP, a method that can help you create an environment within which new insights will be most likely to arise. Before we proceed, however, a word of caution. You may recall our earlier discussion that simply "feeling" you know the best solution to an ethical problem does not necessarily mean that it will be the right thing to do. In the heat of the moment, it is possible to mistake your biases and prejudices for objective fact, for example. And just ask the CEO who testifies that "I never expected this to happen" when some ethical mishap transpires on his or her watch; it is also possible to misread cues, consciously or unconsciously, avoiding that which would cause pain or discomfort. Sadly, there are leaders who regularly confuse fear and greed with listening to their guts, making decisions based on immediate concerns of self-preservation or gratification. Others, equally convinced they are doing what's best for the company, are actually making safe or unnecessarily compromising decisions in the name of expediency.

One of the reasons some leaders fall into these traps is because they mistake an excess of "busyness" with productivity. In reality, it may be a temptation for some to keep working non-stop specifically because when they pause, their consciences have the opportunity to be heard. They may not like what their inner voices are saying, so they do everything they can to override their gut instincts. Know, however, that your values will persist in trying to break through to you. Instinctively understanding the connection between your personal ethics, organizational goals and results, your intuition is constantly whispering in the wings, urging you towards alignment. *Here's what's really going on. This doesn't feel right. Haven't you missed something? Can you really live with this?* Ignore your intuition at your own peril, for truth will make itself known by ensuring that sooner or later, external events will get the attention your internal warning systems could not. Even if you don't like what your gut is trying to tell you, isn't it better to know what you are really dealing with earlier on, when you will be more likely to be able to do something about it, rather than to be overtaken somewhere down the road by "bad luck?" On the flip side, there are solutions waiting to be found, satisfying connections to be made and a better grasp of the situation to be had. Internal resources are inside of you right now, working constantly for you on your behalf, just waiting to be tapped.

A rule of thumb

There is a rule of thumb you can follow if you don't want avoidable surprises to happen to you. Pay attention to your intuition, tell the truth about what you are hearing and trust your instincts. Intuition will work for you to the exact degree to which you have done the hard work of surfacing, clarifying and committing to your own core values. This includes your most deeply held sense of how things ought to be, and assumes that how you believe things ought to be is good. Not only must you become aware of what you deem inwardly to be important, but you must allow yourself to be tested both on the job and in your life over and over again, checking your values, actions and results against humanity's higher rather than lower aspirations. You learn more about yourself every time you set your intention to be honest and courageous, and become willing to engage with whatever arises. It takes courage to be this open to your authentic experience, particularly when it comes to the matter of ethics. *What's really important? What is acceptable to me—and what is not? What constitutes my definition of a successful outcome?* When you have a firm grasp of your own values, you will be able to flow your standards throughout your organization spontaneously. Equally important, when you pay attention to your intuition, there will be a consistency in your behavior—an alignment between who you are at your deepest levels and how you operate at work and in life. This is no less a matter than coming to know yourself.

Having progressed this far, you are learning when and how to tune into your uneasy feelings, trusting that there are times to push through the fear and discomfort that spontaneously arise and proceed anyway—and times to stop and pay apt attention. You have thought about the meaning of your life and work—when and where to draw the ethical line you quite simply will not cross. You are taking the time to get to know the deepest nuances of your rich, inner terrain. In short, you are not only learning to know yourself—but to trust yourself.

By investing this time in your development as a moral agent, you will be able to make better decision when you have the time to go through decision-making processes such as LEAP. Perhaps even more importantly, your decisions will be of a higher quality even when you find yourself having to make a split-second decision in a crisis, unable to go through a methodical assessment of the facts. Taking time to access your intuition can be the one last drop that will make the water flow over the dam. Are you ready?

LEAP: Access Your Intuition Process

Consciously accessing your intuition may be new to you. But even leaders who already trust their intuition will benefit from a simple process that helps them create the environment in which insights, enhanced perspective and breakthroughs are most likely to occur. In this process, you don't need to be surrendering and accepting, or rational and practical. Now you are being asked to use everything you've got: your whole human potential.

In a moment, you will be guided to answer each of nine questions in an unusual way. We'd like you to "follow" rather than lead your thoughts, by writing down everything that comes into your mind without self-censorship or editing. Your words may come out jumbled and wander or jump from subject to subject. Do your best to keep up, writing down faithfully as if taking dictation from the voice in your head. If what you are thinking is, "This is a stupid question!", you would write: "This is a stupid question!" If you are stuck, take the pen and move it to your recessive hand and write about how that feels. Do not stop to think or worry about whether what you are writing is logical or to correct grammatical mistakes. Do not anticipate what is coming next. Keep writing non-stop at least two or three minutes on each before moving on to the next. Finally, resist the urge to read ahead, as these questions are particularly powerful in the sequence presented

Please note that if you already have a solution in mind to the ethical challenge you are facing, it is still important to use this process to help you discern whether or not there's anything you've missed, and to test your solution against your gut. Otherwise, use this in a final no-holds-barred attempt to discover what it is that you ought to do now.

1. What issue or problem would you most like to resolve right now?

2. What outcome would you most like to achieve?

3. How have you tried to resolve this situation so far?

4. What was it about this approach that did not work?

5. What can you change about this situation?

6. What must you accept about this situation?

7. What is your greatest concern about this situation?

8. What is the truth about this situation?

It is highly recommended that you take a break right now between questions 8 and 9 and go somewhere where you can be quiet and alone for at least half an hour. Go for a walk, if possible, taking your mind off of conscious reflection about the issue at end. Do not "try" to get the answer you are looking for. When you come back, resume with question nine.

9. What one thing do you now know you ought to do to get the resolution you seek?

Conclusion

If you have been honest, done all of the internal as well as external homework prescribed in this book, you will have your answer. Your answer may come in the form of the solution to your problem—or it may come in the form of admitting to yourself that you need to go back to the previous steps of LEAP and fill in important pieces you've missed. Perhaps, such as in the case of the search for a site for London's third airport, you realize that you need to collect more, better data. Or perhaps, in your particular case, your gut is telling you that you are on the right track, but that you will need more than a half hour to mull. Perhaps, too, you realize that in this particular circumstance, there quite simply is no perfect solution and that the time has come to move ahead, understanding as fully as possible the risks and consequences as well as the trade-offs and rewards. Whatever the next step is for you, you may not like it, but you are already too well informed and honest to sweep away what others can ignore, rationalize, or simply avoid. By now, you know that the most important ethical question is not *what do I feel like doing*, but rather, *what ought I to do?* As soon as you have the answer to this question, it is time to implement your decision, trusting that given the hard work, courage and discipline you have brought to bear upon the issue during this as well as the previous two steps, you will have arrived at the solution most likely to bring about the best outcome possible.

Put Your Decision to the Test
Step Four of LEAP

Now you know what you ought to do. The seminal question is: *Will you do it? Trust, Inc.* has systematically walked you through all the considerations, factors and processes you need to make a decision that is in alignment with your own values, your organization's goals and the best possible outcomes for stakeholders. Having come this far, you have everything you need to "do" trust. But it must be duly recognized that there are others who have also had access to respectable decision-making methods and yet who have made poor choices—including the failure to act at all.

Periodically throughout the pages of this book, we have made note of the forces and temptations that press upon our contemporary workplaces. There is unprecedented pressure on us to make the numbers, even as we face diminishing resources. We are forced to compete with companies willing to take ethical shortcuts, tempting us to compromise our values to keep up. And, too, there is unrestrained applause for individuals who have turned greed into a high art. Sadly, it has become obvious to us that in some circles, there is the unquestioned belief that breaches of trust come as an inevitable part of the territory. As daily headlines reveal, many leaders are dangerously close to buying their own excuses when it comes to the violation of values and trust, all rationalized in the name of being realistic or competitive.

Hesitating at the portal

It is not only the overtly greedy and dishonest who hesitate at the portal of doing the right thing, however. Even good people can be tempted to go back to the drawing board one more time, to see if there isn't some less painful or risky solution than the one that has emerged so far. If you find yourself hesitating at this juncture, there may be good reason. Striving to merit trust often entails some degree of discomfort. For instance, you may have found it impossible to come up with a solution in which all stakeholders can come out with what they want. You may even be in the difficult position of having to disappoint one or more groups with legitimate interests and arguments in order to serve what you identify to be the greater good. Perhaps, too, you have come face to face with competing goals held by equally passionate and well-argued factions within your organization itself, opening up the possibility for rifts that may not be easily mended. Finally, you may be in a situation where you are right to be concerned that in taking an unpopular but ethically correct stand, your future with your organization may be impacted or even, in an extreme case, at stake. No wonder it is so often tempting to look for an easier way. Perhaps you could just wait it out. Maybe you'll think of something better later.

Integrity a risk worth taking

But the bad news is: not acting bears consequences, as well. Of course, we are all aware of the increasingly common portrait of the formerly revered organizational executive making his or her appearance on the nightly news in pinstripes—and handcuffs. This is but the tip of the iceberg of reasons why once you know what you ought to do, it's worth risking the consequences of following through. On an organizational level, doing the right thing bears a direct benefit to your bottom line over time, by reducing the costs associated with litigation, lobbying and regulation, not to mention savings related to the retention of crisis public relations services. On the proactive side, the ability for you and your marketing department to tell a strong values story—demonstrated not just by codes and mission statements but by specific, tangible actions—will build goodwill with consumers, suppliers and others who can help advance the organization's goals. As an added benefit, the more respected the company, the lower the turnover and the easier the recruitment. In a survey of CEOs attending the World Economic Forum, the majority emphasized the value of a corporation's reputation, going so far as to consider it a more important measure of success than stock performance, profitability, and return on investment. "The reputation of a company and its products used to be regarded as an intangible asset that was very hard to quantify," said John Graham, CEO of Fleishman-Hillard, the communications company that administered the survey. "Business leaders no longer regard traditional financial measures as the ultimate indicator of a company's success."

The reputation for holding and acting on strong values also plays a critical role in your organization's relationship with the financial community, making or breaking your ability to access capital in times of need or opportunity. Judith had an experience with this when she took on a turn-around project as acting CEO for a company in financial jeopardy. It soon became obvious to her that the logical first step was to contact the company's bankers, transforming their antagonistic stance into a collaborative approach, working together toward restructuring the debt. With due diligence, she collected all the numbers and made honest projections, putting all the financial facts on the table. Against the odds, the presentation got a serious hearing, the banker commenting: "We appreciate your candor. Other people have all the right words—but it's obvious they're simply dancing." Ironically, by exposing the very numbers the previous management had attempted to obscure, Judith helped to create the optimum environment in which the desired outcome could transpire.

On both organizational and personal levels, your reputation for trustworthiness is working for you, on your behalf, all the time. People who resonate with the stances you are known for taking will want to do business with you as well as help you advance your career. You will find yourself naturally aligned with other individuals who share your values.

Economic benefit to society

Beyond the goodwill your ethical actions create for your organization as well as your career, there is a benefit in regards to the economic welfare of society, as a whole. In his book, *Trust: The Social Virtues and the Creation of Prosperity*, Francis Fukuyama argues that the level of trust inherent in a society is the single most persuasive factor influencing a nation's economic well being. Fukuyama observes that when a nation or society permits and supports a high level of trust, prosperity and high economic results are likely to follow. In an economy based on trust, such as ours, the rising tide of values is a positive force. It raises all boats.

Recalling the ethical theories that were summarized in the first chapter, you will recognize these arguments for the advancement of values to be largely utilitarian in nature: weighing the consequences in terms of what you believe will do the greatest good for the greatest number of people. Whichever theory you tend to reflect in your approach to ethics, however, there is an argument that can be made for acting on your decision, even if it does entail an element of risk. If you are a deontologist, for example, you will recognize the importance of following through on your decision simply because it is the right thing to do. You believe that you have the moral obligation to listen to your conscience. Practitioners of character ethics would agree with your thinking on this, adding that your greatest happiness will come about as a by product of the nurturing of the highest expression of your human potential, in this case, following through with what you know you ought to do. Ethical egoists, too, can choose to take the high road, finding personal gratification in having done so.

Unwanted consequences

Whatever the theory that urges you forward to act on your best solution, understand, however, that paying heed to your convictions may require something more of you than you wished you'd have to give. It is painful to consider making a decision that you know will bring you face-to-face with the potential for unavoidable or unwanted consequences. It is even more painful when you know that there have been others, faced with similar issues and circumstances, who have taken shortcuts around integrity, appearing at least in the short-term to advance their organizations or careers.

The *I Ching*, the 3000-year-old work of wisdom to which the ancient Chinese philosopher, Confucius, turned for inspiration, equates individuals with flawed integrity who nevertheless seem to be getting ahead, with the apparent triumph of the swamp plant, which grows fabulously tall overnight, attracting the attention of all who pass. Nearby, deep within the soil, a tiny acorn sends up a tender shoot. Which plant, over time, contains the greater potential for success? Come back tomorrow morning and you will see that the swamp plant is already dead. And the acorn? It is growing into a mighty oak—its development destined to influence the landscape of the entire region. As it grows, the acorn is not aware of doing something great—it is merely doing what's next. So it is for ethical leaders, who simply do what they must, decision by decision. Along the way, you become the kind of leader who comes to stand for something, discovering an authenticity, a courage, a resourcefulness that are independent of the circumstances facing you. There is tremendous power in this. The *I Ching* comments: "Whenever a feeling is voiced with truth and frankness, whenever a deed is the clear expression of sentiment, a mysterious and far-reaching influence is exerted. At first it acts on those who are inwardly receptive. But the circle grows larger and larger. The root of all influence lies in one's inner being: given true and vigorous expression in word and deed, its effect is great."

Time to act

You are entreated to persevere, using the oak rather than the swamp plant for your inspiration, even if at the moment it feels as though you've got your head stuck in the dirt while those around you are waving their tendrils giddily in the air. Trust that your greatest influence, power, and success will come as a byproduct of your willingness to do the right thing, time after time. As we will explore further in chapter nine, research reveals that individuals who have proven themselves to be capable of thriving even in challenging times, with their integrity and values intact, share traits of resilience in common. When greeted with an obstacle, resilient people take the leap of faith that plunging through to its depths—not by attempting to outwit or skirt around the challenges that lay head of them—is the way to lead.

Once you've arrived at what you believe to be the best solution possible, it is time to act. Putting your convictions to the test, you set forces in motion to operationalize your decision, developing and implementing the plan. The good news is that having come this far already, you have laid the groundwork for knowing what it is you are setting out to achieve as well as what it will take both from you personally and from your organization to see the decision through.

Here, in *Putting your Decision to the Test*, the final step of our process, the key question becomes: *How will you know you've succeeded?* As in the implementation of any organizational plan, it is critical for accountability to be built in so that you can monitor your organization's advancement towards clearly defined goals. *Have we followed through with what we said we'd do? Are things working out the way we planned? Have we proven worthy of the trust others have placed in us?*

Benchmarking trust

Measuring the cumulative effect of your organization's ethical stances over time is just as important as benchmarking progress and results. The Public Relations Coalition, a partnership of 19 major U.S.-based organizations representing corporate public relations, investor relations, public affairs and related communications disciplines, recommends that organizations periodically measure trust, itself, as a means of determining and quantifying the relationship of an organization to its various constituencies.

In its report "Restoring Trust in Business: Models for Action," the Coalition notes, "Research has found that measurement of trust can demonstrate success that equates to the bottom line. Conversely, lack of trust can limit your power to do the things you want to do. Trust measurement can also provide benchmarks that show the value of trust and allow you to know where you are in the continuum of change. In short, if you don't measure trust and apply it to all parts of the organization, you may find that you're not getting the benefits that trust can produce."

There are numerous measurement methods described in the Coalition's report. A company can seek to assess itself and its relationship to its constituencies by surveying its stakeholders, holding focus groups, taking before and after polls and engaging in the broad spectrum of both qualitative and quantitative research techniques. Whichever the method chosen, the Coalition considers it to be critical to analyze the data collected in light of its meaning and implications. *Have the behaviors, programs or activities implemented by an organization changed what people know, what they think about the organization, and how they actually act?* The ethical leader is called upon to make and follow-through on corrective recommendations; and then, at the appropriate juncture, to measure again.

Correcting mid-course

Whether on the micro-level of making an individual ethical decision or on the macro-level of assessing the organization's reputation, the ethical leader must have the honesty, courage and willingness to correct mid-course whenever there are shortfalls, slippages or out-and-out misses. At one time, Carol's public relations agency was handling what was then one of California's leading coaching companies. The rapidly-growing organization, led by a charismatic entrepreneur, provided career and life consulting to mid-level professionals in the throes of career transition. All went well until the recession threw a stick into the gears. Profitability was being negatively impacted and the clients' savings were running dry. Then, Leo, the founder of the company, had what he called a Big Idea. He would start a multi-level marketing business on the side. While getting involved in the vitamin business was meant to be just one option for the clients to consider, the dynamics of his practice had shifted. Subtly feeling the pressure to get on board with the side business, many of the clients felt betrayed. To Leo's credit, as quickly as he had jumped into the vitamin business, he got out, publicly acknowledging that he had inadvertently crossed a line. Originally good intentions were compromised by an admittedly mixed agenda.

In the course of his *mea culpa*, Leo shared a story with his clients and staff that helped to explain the ease with which he self-corrected. Several years prior, Leo had decided to get his pilot's license. During one of his lessons, the instructor told him about one of the plane's features: the autopilot. You program the autopilot with a destination and it is the device's job to keep the airplane on course. What Leo hadn't realized, however, is that the autopilot does not take the plane on a straight path to its objective. In fact, the plane is off-course the majority of the time. What the autopilot does, however, is keep careful track of how off-course the plane is at any given moment—continually making the appropriate corrections. Taking a lesson from the autopilot, not only did Leo drop the vitamin business, but he also added a workshop on entrepreneurialism, providing the opportunity for his clients to consider starting the business of their choice.

Not every course of self-correction goes as smoothly as this, however. There may be those times when situations have definitively gotten out of hand. Sometimes there are external factors, such as "Acts of God" or the quirkiness of human nature, that could not have been anticipated. But there are also those times when you or someone on your team has flat out made a mistake. There may be errors in our calculations, variables that were underestimated and yes, even expediencies that blinded us to what should have been obvious. Here the temptation can be great, indeed, to compound one mistake with another: the urge to cover-up a mis-step in the misguided effort to evade potentially negative consequences. Ironically, daily headlines remind us that when we attempt to avoid our moment of reckoning in order to self-protect, things inevitably get worse for us. Rather, it behooves the ethical leader to readily admit to the mistake, rectify what is possible, and put him or herself to the serious task of setting things right. To do so, it is incumbent upon the leader to spend as little time as possible feeling victimized, accusing others of having caused him or her to go astray, and more time getting on with life.

The ability to stay focused on the goal is exemplified by a story that appeared in the sports pages of a major daily newspaper. When interviewed by a sportswriter, the coach of a major league baseball team was asked to comment on the chances of bringing up a new, promising pitcher from the minors.

"There's plenty of talent in the minors," he commented. "In fact, some of the boys we have on the farm have stronger skills than the ones we've got here. But the thing is, it's not the talent that is the deciding factor in what makes a major league pitcher."

"What is?" asked the columnist.

"It's how well he learns to fail."

The test of leadership is not whether you can stay true to your values when things are going your way—but rather, how you do when the ball you're throwing misses the plate. Often, there is something you can do better next time. Certainly, you learn from the things that happen to and because of you, including your mistakes. But people who learn to fail well understand that while introspection and regret have their place, it's critical to stay focused on making the corrections as quickly as possible, getting you and your organization back on track towards the achievement of your goals.

Of course, ethics is not something that transpires in a vacuum. Your organization's culture plays a critical role in terms of how quickly and efficiently you both implement your plans and self-correct, when necessary. In the next chapter, we will discuss the importance of establishing an environment in which people are most likely to bring their best to work with them, not only in terms of the fulfillment of their own potential—but their ability to contribute to the organization. Bridging the gap between personal values and organizational goals unleashes the power of alignment for unprecedented productivity and heightened employee morale. These aren't just empty words. The ethical leader is willing to put his or her values to the test, not only to resolve the issue at hand—but to build an organization that others can believe in, no matter what.

PART THREE

Leadership Worthy of Respect
Resilience, Ethics and Trust

The Ethical Organization

An ethical organization builds its reputation decision by decision. However, the quality of these decisions will inevitably be influenced by the organizational culture within which they are being made. As the consequences of breaches of trust continue to come to light, management is forced to look beyond mere compliance, making the more daunting effort to do the honest, consistent and fair thing. This has to be built into the very fabric of the organization. As part of this, the relatively new field of business ethics is becoming professionalized as a management discipline, finding its place in organizational life just down the hall from human resources and public relations. Reflecting this phenomenon, the Ethics Officer Association has grown exponentially over the past several years, closing in on a membership of close to 1000 executives, representing hundreds of companies. The formal ethics programs they are implementing use a wide variety of management and training tools and techniques to develop values-based policies and procedures and cultivate behaviors aligned with these values.

But it doesn't take an ethics specialist on the payroll and an official code of conduct posted on the wall for an organization to have and act upon a shared understanding of what is proper organizational behavior—and what is not. In fact, even if an organization has the formal accoutrements of an ethics program in place, the single most important determinant of an organization's approach to ethics will be the CEO's own ethical standards and behavior, supported by the ability and/or willingness to flow his or her values through the company. It is good news, indeed, when the people at the top embody organizational values that advance the corporate culture. They are most likely to succeed on every level—and under every circumstance. However, a large-scale study of organizational life, as reported by Linda Klebe Trevino and Gary R. Weaver, in their book *Managing Ethics in Organizations*, indicates that there is a double edge to this sword. For the research also indicates that "for outcomes to be most positive, employees must perceive that executives and supervisors care about ethics and values as much as they care about the bottom line, and leaders must demonstrate this commitment every day through words and actions." As an example, the authors relate their conversations with mid-level managers and supervisors of a highly regulated company that invested significant resources in the development of a "world class" ethics/compliance program. "The firm's managers reported, however, that at their monthly two hour review meetings with the Chief Operating Officer, 'We spend 5 minutes on compliance and 115 minutes on profitability. So, you tell me—what matters here?'"

The allocation of time only becomes an issue when there is a pre-existing lack of alignment between espoused values and organizational culture. In the best case scenario, mutually understood ethical obligations are woven into the fabric of the organization. Every decision refers back to expectations and looks ahead to accountability. Discussions organically and unselfconsciously begin with both the CEO and the team's commitment to the organization's highest standards, aligning profit goals with these integrated values. Ideally, the line between ethics and operations virtually disappears when trust is given.

Recently, Carol brought up the issue of organizational culture with the members of her ethics class of adult doctoral students in organizational leadership, many of whom have key positions in major corporations. Several who work for the same ethically challenged company placed the blame for their company's problems on "just a couple of bad apples in sales, spoiling things for the rest of us." Later, one of the students came to Carol privately and brought up a troubling issue that he thought to be entirely unrelated. The company had recently instituted an honor code that he had felt pressured by his boss to sign. "I'm not concerned that there will be any of the big headline-making stuff in this division, but I do think it's hypocritical to speak in terms of acting in accordance with our company's lofty values, when my boss thinks nothing of stealing credit for the work I do, playing favorites with his yes-men and telling us that we should do whatever it takes to make our numbers." He went on to explain that at the very same time the boss was pushing for numbers, there were individuals he'd kept around who ought to have been released long ago. Clearly, the boss lacked the courage to act with integrity, undermining the other employees' trust and loyalty. The demoralized division deeply resented having to work double-time to make up for both these individuals' and their boss' lack of competency, not to mention moral fiber.

And the one bad apple? Suddenly, the student who had previously thought of the ethical breaches at his company as isolated incidents, recognized that they were, instead, only one example. More extreme manifestations on a continuum of distrust and disloyalty had weakened the fabric of ethics throughout the organization. To get a better grasp on why so many companies with ethics programs are still getting into trouble for what is, at first glance, the indiscretions of a handful of opportunists, one needs only turn to the numbers concerning employee attitudes about their bosses. The global human capital and financial management consulting firm Watson Wyatt issued an Employee Attitudes and Opinions Survey on the subject, providing evidence that in the majority of workplaces surveyed, employees clearly feel compromised by day-to-day hypocrisy and broken promises. According to their study of company CEOs and top managers by employees, 62 percent were accused of hypocrisy, 60 percent of favoritism and 53 percent of dishonesty.

It is relatively easy to publish conduct policies and to bring in an outside ethics trainer for a brown bag lunch. But the creation of a values-driven organization is an on-going process, requiring vision, courage and follow-through, not only from the top down, but from the inside out. Following are three tasks we have deemed critical for the ethical leader who is serious about the creation of an environment in which individuals can reach their highest ethical potential.

The creation of meaning

Human beings are meaning-making creatures. Unlike other living organisms that concern themselves primarily with the business of everyday life, simply responding to their survival needs, we want our lives to be about something. Understanding this, the best leaders not only provide their employees with the means to make a living—but with recognition concerning the meaning of their work, itself. A sense of purpose doesn't need to be grand—such as working together to put an astronaut on Mars. It is enough to create an environment in which people know they will be treated fairly, that the values of the company are not just lip service, and that the company "really means it" when it broadcasts that for which it stands.

The obvious prerequisite for the creation of meaning is that the organizational leader has taken the time and made the effort to figure out what gives his or her own life, work and career meaning. Only then can there be a consistent center around which others may rally. Become such a source of meaning, and your reports will instinctively understand where you are coming from and where you are heading the organization. They will know what it means to be part of the team, with clear expectations and consistent accountability. When they come to work every day, they will relish the sense that they can "be themselves," with their values at home and their values at work in alignment. This is a happy outcome for new hires. It takes root at the very beginnings of the relationship. Organizational values and expectations are spelled out in recruitment ads and interviews, reinforced by new employee and refresher training programs, reflected consistently in messages and through the actions as well as words of mentors, role models and peers. Because everyone in the organization is working from the same page, your organization will become respected for its ability and willingness to tell the truth and to deal with real issues. Suppliers will be selected and groomed on the basis of their willingness to align themselves with the organization's standards. Stakeholders both within and outside your organization will find their association with you to be a source of pride.

The leader who proves him or herself worthy of this level of respect becomes a force for the good. When times are difficult, the values-driven leader holds firm against the pressures of opposing forces, be it the temptation to cut ethical corners in order to make a profit, to put off implementing costly corrections that he or she knows are necessary, or to cover up admitting to having made a mistake. One such leader is Bill George, the CEO who grew the medical device maker, Medtronic, from $755 million in annual sales and 4000 employees to a $5.5 billion company with 26,000 on its payroll. Shortly after he left the company, he described becoming such a caretaker of his company's highest aspirations in an article that appeared in *Fortune* magazine. He writes: "I can't imagine telling a worker at Medtronic she needed to make the best pacemaker she could to please Wall Street—or for that matter to please the company's shareholders. What does my employee care about some fund manager or trader? She doesn't. So what does motivate her?"

George once asked a Medtronic worker who was making heart valves that very question. "I'm making these valves to save lives," she responded. "I'm saving 1,000 lives a year. And if I make one bad valve, someone is going to die." By his own account, George learned the importance of what she was saying the hard way. "Soon after joining the company, I was visiting a doctor performing an angioplasty procedure with a Medtronic balloon catheter to open up clogged arteries. The product literally fell apart in the doctor's hands as he was threading it through the patient's arteries. He was so angry that he took the catheter, covered with blood, and threw it at me. I ducked as it went sailing across the room."

Because the leader who values trust knows how things ought to be, he or she is devoted to getting all the pieces into alignment—not just the obvious ones close to the bone of the organization, but the ones pressing in from the outside, and the ones that are apt to go untended at the bottom. When Judith took over responsibility for supervision of the flight attendants for TWA, one of the first things she did was open her office door, asking crew members as they happened to pass by to come in for a minute. She took the opportunity to invite their opinions about how things were going, asking for suggestions and brainstorming in terms of improvements in areas that directly affected their experience on the job. The flight attendants responded positively, pleased to be consulted. Even when an individual's good idea could not be implemented readily, Judith kept her in the loop, reporting back with periodic progress reports.

Judith's belief in the creation of individual meaning proved to have empirical value when she turned her attention to solving the problem of absenteeism by flight crew members during the winter holidays. Typically, as many as one third of the 56 flight attendants in the region could be expected to call in sick over the popular vacation period, abandoning their posts in favor of personal time with family and friends. Various punishments and rewards had been tried in the past, to no avail. What else could the organization try? Judith recalled a lesson she'd learned watching her father operate his little automotive supplies business. Her father would address the salespeople: "Yes sir, No sir." One day, the young Judith asked him: "You are the boss. They should be calling you 'sir', not the other way around. Why do you treat them like this?" He replied: "It's the right thing to do. You give each individual respect for the role he or she is playing. We're all in this together, just called upon to do different jobs."

Thinking about her father's words, Judith realized that the absenteeism problem was not an issue to be addressed through the revamping of organizational systems, but rather an opportunity for cultivating mutual respect and trust. Judith decided then and there to write a personal holiday card to each of the flight attendants on the team, telling her how much she counted on her personally and how important her individual contribution was in regards to keeping the system running, especially during such a critical time of year. That holiday season, not one of the 56 called in sick. Providing feedback at the end of the holiday crunch, the flight attendants connected the dots for management, reiterating how good it felt to be counted upon to assume their share in the responsibility for optimum operation of the airline, simultaneously expressing gratitude that someone had noticed.

The establishment of trust through open communication

The making of meaning is dependent upon the establishment of trust. Trust, in turn, is cultivated by open communications throughout the organization, with two-way channels permanently set in the on position. Employees know that you are available to them on whatever issue arises along the way. In the best organizations, there's no need for an official open door policy because the door is never closed.

Again, it's one thing to say that an organization has adopted open communications in its operations, it's another thing for the CEO or manager to take the time to listen when someone actually brings up an issue, especially one that wasn't already on the leader's agenda. It may be painful and time-consuming to hear complaints about favoritism and elitism, broken promises and role conflict. You may be forced to confront issues that were not previously on your radar screen: a lack of alignment between reward systems and espoused values, for example. You may find it uncomfortable to openly discuss issues of compensation, including your own, and to speak candidly with employees and stakeholders about your values. Once you've given the permission to put things up to question, the leader had better be ready to respond thoughtfully and authentically to whatever arises.

The true measure of a leader is when he or she turns the corner from resisting challenges on such matters and actually becomes glad that people in the organization trust him or her enough to pick up the phone and say "We've got a problem here." Or better still: to make the call before the problem has even had the opportunity to manifest itself. The leader who runs a trust-based organization considers bad news to be a negative only if it's not dealt with. One way to ensure that open communication is more than lip service is to put in place a fair treatment policy, guaranteeing employees in the organization the procedural right to be heard by management, going as high up the chain of command as necessary, including the CEO. Ethical hot lines, too, provide a means of surfacing uncomfortable information. However, we believe that if an organization needs to rely on providing the protection of anonymity as the solution to the individual employee's concerns about retribution, there is critical work to be done on the culture, overall.

Trust is imperative in regard to employees but must extend beyond the walls to all stakeholders in organizational life, including, or perhaps particularly, the investors. In the PR Coalition's study, "Restoring Trust in Business," the authors write: " Some companies will be leaders in making information available to investors. Others will reluctantly comply with these new rules as their lawyers counsel that being too progressive involves too much risk." The study argues that it is in management's best interest to provide board members all relevant analysts reports, favorable and unfavorable, and let them see the most frequently asked questions from analysts or institutional investors. For this and related reasons, the PR Coalition makes a recommendation with which we concur: that the chief public relations officer report directly to the CEO on matters having to do with the public's perception of corporate leadership. If the organization "really means it," this will not be a matter of smoke and mirrors—but rather, a way to proactively seek out early notice of potential problems. In such an environment, critics are engaged rather than avoided, the organization trusting that open communication at every stage along the way with all constituencies provides all interested parties with the greatest potential for a successful outcome.

While the ethical leader does the right things for the right reasons, the fact is that there are empirical benefits that are a byproduct of this, going straight to the bottom line. Watson Wyatt's 2001/2002 Human Capital Index study found that companies with the best human capital strategies—including effective communications—had a three times greater return to shareholders over five years than companies with the worst strategies. Findings indicate that a company that improves communications integrity—creating an environment where employees can and will share their knowledge—can grow market value 7.1 percent.

Forging "a custodial chain of integrity"

We come now to the third of the organizational leader's three tasks. In the previous task, we addressed the importance of welcoming rather than resisting challenging information. Now, we take this to an even deeper level, intentionally seeking root causes for ethical issues, and attending to the details before they turn into big events. The details may seem small, but in the context of the ethical organization, they are everything. In fact, it is rare for an individual act to make or break a company's reputation. More often, the dramatic breaches of trust that make headline news begin more subtly as hairline cracks, manifesting themselves in such routine occurrences as an exaggeration in a report, or an exception to a policy. For example, take the case of the disgruntled employee with a gun in his briefcase who somehow makes it past the security checkpoint at city hall. Somebody whose responsibility it is to check out everybody who enters the building allowed that employee around the metal detector. This can't be an isolated incident, but rather, the symptom of a complacency that sets all too easily into the daily routines of workplace life. The security guard took his job—as well as a gunman—for granted, and now an innocent person lay on the floor of an upstairs office, gunned down in the prime of life.

As this apocryphal story illustrates, trust is not to be confused with familiarity or complacency, but is something far more profound. The expectation is that all employees, from the mailroom clerk to the CEO, understand that it is part of one's job description that he or she build trust with him or herself, as well as with others, by consistently acting honestly, taking the time to get to the real bottom of issues and finding the courage to take unpopular stands. When the organization has made trust a core value, each individual strives to be worthy of the trust that others have invested in him or her. Each and every individual in, connected with or impacted by an organization—each and every decision, behavior and act—is part of a complex web of relationships. Everyone is charged with the responsibility to be ever mindful of the chain of integrity, stepping forward and being responsible for his or her part in aligning action with organizational values every single time. When the account executive puts together her expense report, she is honest. When the bill goes to the client, it is accurate. When the shipping dispatcher agrees to get a package to a customer on time, it's out the door at the appointed hour. And these are not special cases to be singled out for applause. Rather, these are the kinds of things that individuals in the organization do routinely, when they are rushed, when they are tired, when they are pressured because attention to the chain of integrity has become a habit.

Robert Galford and Anne Seibold Drabeau in a February 2003 article in *Harvard Business Review* titled "The Enemies of Trust" write: "If people trust each other and their leaders, they'll be able to work through disagreements. They'll take smarter risks. They'll work harder, stay with the company longer, contribute better ideas, and dig deeper than anyone has a right to ask." This is the kind of place the best prospective employees are looking for when they say they want to go to work for a "good company." They know that in such an environment, there is going to be less time second-guessing their boss, playing politics and sorting out the rumors from the facts. They know they will be treated fairly, and that their contributions will be valued. Spending less of its resources on the time and costs associated with litigation, crisis public relations and high-priced faux accounting practices, the ethical organization can devote its best energy and significant investment of resources to advance rather than protect the organization. The employees feel secure in their own as well as their organization's future. They are inspired to bring their best, rather than their worst, to work with them every day.

In the end, the leader committed to building trust will discover something that has the potential to be truly transformative: that there is no such thing as an ethical organization. There are only human beings in organizations acting ethically.

Resilience for Challenging Times

Making a tough ethical decision can be difficult under the best of circumstances. But in times of intense societal change such as our own, the challenges—and stakes—are even higher. What does it mean to operate in a global economy, for instance, in a world where issues of power and control are fought out at the national, regional and even tribal levels? Science and technology, too, are forcing many ethical leaders onto unexplored territory. It may be acceptable to transplant a heart, for example—but how about a head? And, too, what are the long-range implications of genetic research on our food chain and artificial intelligence on the defense industry? Even in traditional industries and fields, there are changing rules, standards and interpretations of the law. In light of Sarbanes-Oxley, for instance, to whom does the lawyer, the accountant, the management consultant owe his or her allegiance? Confidentialities which were once kept as a testimony to the highest professional ethics are now vulnerable to being breached in the name of a greater good. Who do we trust? To whom and to what are we responsible? *How ought we to lead?*

It wasn't that long ago when leaders could more often than not white-knuckle it through the difficult times, relying on motivational pep talks and the promise of a brighter future to give them strength. Now, there is the growing suspicion that learning to deal with change and uncertainty in our work lives is not an exception to the rule, but a fact of life. We may still have the urge to do business as usual—but how do you define "usual" when the status quo is, itself, in a state of flux? No wonder as the new millennium was getting underway, *Harvard Business Review* noted that "Resilience is a hot topic in business these days." The increasing fascination with resilience is of more than academic interest as even the casual observer can see. Some people resist the pressures to compromise or self-delude in the face of societal forces and temptations while others routinely succumb to the unethical. What separates those individuals and organizations who resist from those who succumb?

As we discussed in the last chapter, one obvious clue is the degree to which values have been built into a given organization. Are the ethics flowing from the top down—and are both the espoused and enacted ethics of that organization aligned with the individual's own deepest sense of how he or she ought to live? If so, the individual in that organization will be making his or her ethical decisions within an environment conducive to making work an expression of basic human goodness. But even in a well-run organization, the possibility always exists that a particular individual will be having a harder time with this than others.

Psychologist Abraham Maslow laid the groundwork for a reasonable explanation for variations in human behavior in his pyramidal hierarchy of human needs. In brief, Maslow's research proposed that people's integrity is impacted by the circumstances they face. Those who are at the bottom of the pyramid—representing the broadest segment of the population—are those who are dealing with issues of survival. Individuals who are consumed with worrying about their next meal, are not likely to be thinking about abstract philosophical issues, such as the meaning of goodness and beauty, right and wrong.

Maslow aside, it is obvious that there are some leaders who, far from being in physical jeopardy, live in big houses, take luxurious trips, drive fancy cars and nevertheless live as though their survival is at stake. People who perceive themselves to be fighting for their very existence, experiencing their lives as if they were at the bottom of the pyramid, say things like: *It's us or them; I'm on my own on this; You can't trust anybody*, and *This is a dog-eat-dog world*. We have known organizational bullies who to the outside world appear to be in positions of power, but who regularly operate on the border of physical abuse, slamming doors and overturning chairs in childlike tantrums. This behavior is of the lowest order possible: the ability to survive—but not to thrive. Research suggests that the higher up you go on the pyramid, the less consumed with reactive, self-protective issues of survival you become. At some point, as you become sufficiently self-aware of your own values, concepts like honor and ethics take on authentic meaning for you. At the top of the pyramid, a peak reserved for the likes of Mahatma Gandhi, Eleanor Roosevelt and Martin Luther King, Jr. resilience goes resolutely beyond survival of the fittest. At the peak, we become known for our ability to hold onto our values no matter what.

But aside from a handful of saints, merely having attained a higher perch on the pyramid at some point in your life does not assure that you will never slip back down should the heat be turned up. Is it a coincidence, for instance, that ethical breaches making headline news soared shortly after the tragedy of 9/11, both fueling and reflecting fears related to terrorism and market instability? Job insecurity, an increasingly competitive global marketplace, wild swings in the stock market, the loss of personal savings as well as the collapse of the financial institutions, themselves, all take their toll on individuals who may find themselves slipping down the pyramid towards survival mode. At the same time, there have always been exceptions to the rule. There are people who act out of the highest human potentialities even when in the challenging position of dealing with objective matters of survival. Researchers have studied teenagers in gang-infested communities who have resisted joining up, elderly widowers who have retained positive attitudes about life despite the loss of their beloved spouses, and Holocaust victims who have survived unspeakable tragedy. It is testimony to the true human potential that there will always be those who manage to retain their values to find continued meaning in their lives regardless of the circumstances they face.

One such individual was Ishi, the last Native American of his tribe. In the early 1900s, Ishi made a momentous decision. After living alone for some time, having watched his entire tribe succumb one by one to the ravenous appetites of the coyotes and wolves of Northern California, he suddenly appeared one day at dawn in downtown Oroville, California. Not knowing what to think of this strange naked man, the people of Oroville quickly clothed him and put him in jail. When the Bureau of Indian Affairs was contacted, Ishi's story hit the San Francisco dailies. Among those reading about Ishi was the anthropologist Alfred Kroeber. Kroeber decided to bring Ishi to the museum at the University of California by train. As the train pulled into the station in Oroville, Ishi quietly hid behind a cottonwood tree alongside the platform. His traveling companions beckoned to him, and together they boarded the train.

Some time later, after they had become good friends, Kroeber asked Ishi what he'd been afraid of. Ishi replied that he and his tribe had been aware of the train all his life, but they had all assumed it to be a demon that ate people. They had watched it bellowing and smoking, and had seen people swallowed up within it never to emerge again. Kroeber listened to Ishi, wonder flooding over him. At last, he asked, "How did you have the courage to just get on the train if you thought it was a demon?" Ishi answered, "My life has taught me to be more curious than afraid."

The key to Ishi's resilience seemed to those who knew him to be his infectious curiosity. He had an openness, a willingness to try new things and ways of being that was greater than any of the fears he may have been feeling. Moreover, he knew who he was. He had an integrity that allowed him to interact with forces outside of himself without changing anything essential about himself. This was his source of power.

Ishi's qualities of resilience seemed innate, but they can also be learned. Among Carol's coaching clients was Hal, a production manager employed by a direct mail cataloger. Hal was a hard-working employee who anticipated what was needed of him and performed consistently beyond expectations. But Hal had some concerns about certain corporate practices that he decided to keep to himself. Because he had been taught that if you want to get ahead, don't rock the boat, he was sure that if he expressed his concerns, he would not be viewed as a team player and would be passed over for promotion. When an opportunity for advancement opened up, the company shocked Hal by announcing that it was going outside the organization to search for someone who could bring new ideas and leadership to the business—precisely what Hal had been holding back. At this point, what did Hal have to lose? Taking a deep breath, he took the risk of telling his boss his honest opinions. The boss was silent for a long moment. Then, at last, he spoke. "I had no idea you were thinking about these things. That's just the kind of feedback we're looking for." Hal got the promotion, realizing that his long-practiced urge to self-protect was the very thing that had blocked his progress. In his new position, he began challenging himself and others to share more of their authentic thoughts and feelings with one another: to take the risk of closing the gap between their personal values and organizational goals. Working in this new mode, Hal blossomed, rising to the senior level of management. Authenticity gradually became a habit for him and his team, contributing to the growth of the company.

Ironically, it was the company's success that was to put Hal's resilience to its greatest test. As it turned out, the company had become an attractive candidate for acquisition. In fact, as a lucrative deal was consummated, Hal's boss was offered a generous buy-out on his contract and Hal suddenly had a new boss, someone he had not previously known. Systems began undergoing dramatic change and in fact, some of the same questionable practices that Hal had managed to expose earlier were being re-introduced. Hal spoke up, but this time the results were drastically different. His new boss accused him of disloyalty, warning him to keep his thoughts to himself. Having discovered his own innate power, including an unshakable trust in himself and his values, Hal immediately began making plans to leave. The last time Carol spoke with Hal, he shared that what he once viewed as a catastrophe—the loss of his job—now seemed like a great adventure. At the top of his networking list: his former boss who had recently taken a position with an even larger catalogue company.

Hal and Ishi's resilience derived from their authenticity: the willingness to take a risk that their greatest potential for happiness would come not despite their core values, but because of them. The studies of resilient people reveal a number of traits held in common.

THREE MAIN TRAITS OF RESILIENT LEADERS

1. A commitment to truth telling

Can you be counted on to be honest with yourself? Maslow referred to this quality as "Reality-Centered"—the ability to differentiate the artificial or superficial from the authentic and genuine. Resilient people differentiate themselves from those who become victimized by life's circumstances through the stripping away of false notions about the situation they face in order to deal with what is real.

There is a wonderful story from the Buddhist tradition that illustrates this quality. A monk, seeking the key to enlightenment, sat still in contemplation in the temple garden. As he sat, a maple leaf broke free from a tree nearby and floated gently to the ground. The monk bowed in homage to the leaf that had showed him how effortlessly it shared both its front and its back side as it fell, hiding nothing. No secrets, no denial, no excuses. That is what truth telling is all about: seeing the back side of the situations with which we are faced as an integral part of the whole. People who do not want to see the back side of the situations they face in their lives settle for the superficial. How do they do this? There are many ways. They can be in denial, pretending that things are better than they are. They can rationalize waiting it out. They can work so hard that they don't have time to think. And, too, they can sufficiently dull their capacity to tell the truth with alcohol, drugs or any manner of excess.

Resilient people do not give into the temptation to deny, avoid or rationalize, knowing that it is only the degree to which they are willing to face the real issues, that they can do something genuine about it. In the context of ethical decision-making, resilient leaders resist the tendency to admit only to the things that will be easiest to fix, instead seeking out and addressing root causes.

2. Dedication to values

Commitment to truth telling is a prerequisite to ethical leadership, particularly in times of intense societal change. However, given the volume of data that pours into us everyday, how can we possibly be clear headed enough to call upon the most productive resources and come to the best solutions? The answer, in brief, is that for resilient people, values serve as the organizing principle. This is particularly important at those times when the demands of the moment press the leader to make split second decisions. At those times—whether pressed or not—ethical issues are at stake.

Judith had an experience of this early in her career, when she was the first woman at TWA to be moved out of what was then a traditional job for women—working with flight attendants—and into management. Her new peers, all men, were not thrilled with the prospect of welcoming a woman into their ranks. Things came to a head for Judith when her team was called upon to come up with a plan for TWA to improve the delivery time for bags at O'Hare Airport. While the rest of the team took an adversarial position of management versus the baggage department, Judith suggested that they take a collaborative approach. Why not get the union involved and get their help in solving the problem?

Judith, having always been held in high esteem by her co-workers, was caught off guard. She thought of herself as a manager, not a woman manager. And so when she did not receive invitations to important meetings, was frozen out of decision-making processes, and criticized for her collaborative management style, she came to the logical, but inaccurate, conclusion that she must be doing something wrong. Did she ask too many questions? Was it naïve to trust and respect her subordinates? Did her emphasis on the quality of her relationships make her look weak?

Around that time, she read an article in *Harvard Business Review* on the notion of problem ownership. When is a problem yours to solve, and when have you taken on something that belongs to somebody else? As she recalls it, referring to problems that belong to somebody else, the article warned "Don't take on that monkey." Suddenly, she realized that she had, indeed, taken on a monkey that did not belong to her. Simply stated, her co-workers did not respect her management style not because there was anything wrong about her approach—but simply because she was a woman. This, she realized, was not her problem—but theirs. And moreover, she refused to fail because of somebody else's issues. She would hold onto her own core values that expressed themselves through her management style. But she wouldn't take being frozen out passively. She decided to try out a new strategy, one upon which she has relied for the duration of her career: to stick to her core values and trust that in the end, it will have proven to be the right thing to do. In this case, Judith found alignment with a regional VP who recognized her contributions and admired her management style. He encouraged the team to give her collaborative approach a try. The result: the team shared in the praise as by implementing Judith's plan. TWA had the best baggage delivery statistics to date.

3. The willingness to take a stand

Resilient people consistently show themselves to be willing to sacrifice personal comfort and safety in order to act in accordance with what they believe to be the right thing to do. In times of adversity, this willingness to take a stand provides the solid ground upon which one may face circumstances firmly and steadfastly. At the same time, resilient people know they cannot always get things to turn out for them just the way they want. They cannot always make and carry out a plan that is guaranteed to protect them from pain. When times are tough, they do not take a tailspin into survival mode, trashing their values and integrity at the first sign of trouble. They rely, instead, on their values to get them through the hard times. Rather than allowing fear to debilitate them, they use everything they've got—including their fear—to carry them forward.

We are reminded here of Joseph Campbell's selection of a favorite story from *La Queste del Sainte Graal*, the story of King Arthur's quest for the Holy Grail. In this episode, King Arthur's knights were seated at his table, but Arthur would not let the meal be served until an adventure had occurred. Sure enough, the Grail appeared to them, carried by angelic powers, veiled by cloth. Then, abruptly, it disappeared. Arthur's nephew Gawain proposed that the knights pursue the Grail in order to see it unveiled. So off they went. Campbell's favorite lines were these: "They thought it would be a disgrace to go forth in a group. Each entered the forest that he had chosen where there was no path and where it was darkest."

In times of challenge and change, before you lies uncharted territory. Certain options and possibilities you once thought you had open to you have been closed off, while other routes, some of them leading you deeper into the unknown, beckon to you. *What if I pick the wrong one? Where am I going? What if I end up making a mistake?*

We can take inspiration here from the story of Thor Heyerdahl. Thor was an adventurer who felt called to re-create the voyage he believed the Egyptians to have made across the Atlantic Ocean to South America. While historians ridiculed his theory on the basis that given the technology of the time, such a voyage would have been impossible, Heyerdahl persisted in building a full-size working model of an Egyptian boat and setting forth for South America. Naming his primitive boat, the *Kon Tiki*, Thor managed the journey—overcoming the many obstacles that presented themselves to him along the way. What interests us here most is an observation he made. *The biggest dangers lay close to the shore.* Once he had broken through the shoals and reefs, the expanse of ocean brought "great relief."

Still clinging to the shore, people who call themselves realists complain daily that the values they practice in their personal lives outside of work can't cut it in the pressured environment of our global marketplace. But the true leaders are those of us who defy the odds, figuring out a way to be both authentic and successful. In the long run, resilient people come to stand for something, discovering a vitality, an authenticity, a courage, a resourcefulness that are not dependent on the circumstances facing them. When greeted with obstacles, resilient people take the leap of faith that it will not be by attempting to outwit or skirt around dangers, but by plunging through to their very hearts, that how we ought to lead can be found. Learning to take on the uncertainty and to negotiate life-affirming commitments and relationships, no matter what, is the essence of ethical leadership.

In the end, it is your core values, alone, that can be counted upon to be stronger than fate. To be authentic requires great self-discipline. Not the cracking of the taskmaster's whip. But rather, a dedication to the truth. Genuine authenticity is the act of stripping away false notions about yourself and the situation you face in order to deal with what is real. When you become willing to engage the truth—to clarify your values, to listen to your gut, to bring your best to the challenges you face—you will be among those who thrive no matter what, building rather than breaching trust regardless of the circumstances. While it is true that there are moments when the ethical issues we encounter seem clear, simple and straightforward, it is also true that there will be those occasions when we will be challenged to dig deeper, finding courage, strength and resources we did not know we possessed. As Thor instructs us, it is when we attempt to cling to safety that we are in the greatest peril. Or, as Helen Keller once remarked: "Life is an adventure, or it's nothing."

Every day, newspaper headlines have breaking news about leaders who have breached our trust. We are shocked at the damage that has been done to various stakeholders in their organizations, communities and world—not to mention their personal lives and families. We wonder if we should pull our money out of the market, worrying about who will be next. Corporate leaders who should know better are tragically revealed as having put their own interests ahead of their responsibilities to those who had believed in them. But it isn't only news making leaders at the peak of the hierarchy who make the unfortunate choice to breach rather than build trust.

Typical of the co-authors' experiences is this recent exchange with the training manager of a global company with over 100 offices and thousands of employees around the globe. We were suggesting that they do a training based on the material covered in *Trust, Inc.*

"We don't offer ethics training because we can't afford to take the time away from billable hours," he explained.

"No ethics training is offered whatsoever?" Patiently, we explained to him that we thought of calling him because in a similarly sized and styled firm in the very same industry, a client had recently threatened a lawsuit because of a wide range of ethical breaches by several senior executives, everything from over billing to unrevealed conflicts of interest. Now we were being rushed in to do ethics consulting on the back end, at our higher crisis rates. This expenditure was but a drop in the bucket compared to the cost of legal counsel, lost business and employee turnover related to the case.

"If we were in crisis," he replied, "we would be hiring your services, too."

"Why not do the training in advance, setting the standards, dealing with the issues, before they comprise a crisis?"

"Truthfully," he replied. "I couldn't agree with you more. I know there are issues here. But it would be a risk to even propose ethics training to our CEO. He has made it clear that everything we do here is about pushing every possible dollar through the door. I couldn't justify this to him and I don't want to put my own job at risk."

This, we then understood, was an organization already in breach of trust. Driven by fear, the greater good of the company—let alone of the larger community of stakeholders who have placed their trust in this company—has already been undermined. While the director of training bears responsibility for his unwillingness to buck the system to take the risk of doing the right thing, the ethical flaws in this company had begun at the very top. Unless someone in the organization found the courage to speak up, it would only be a matter of time before we got the call asking for crisis counseling, reading about them in the business section of the daily paper.

Throughout the pages of *Trust, Inc.* we have taken up the gauntlet of teaching organizational leaders committed to both values and results the importance of building rather than breaching trust with stakeholders while going about the day-to-day business of leading their divisions and companies. *Trust, Inc.* argues that leaders who place a high value on operationalizing trust even in the face of adversity can count on players who are on the same page, who have the clarity and courage to address the real root problems and the confidence to dutifully carry through on plans and to seek opportunities to innovate. The pay-off is increased productivity and an enhanced bottom line, as the organization learns to speak and act in alignment.

At the beginning of this book, we asked the question: *Is it possible to be a values-driven leader and still succeed in the pressured environment of the contemporary workplace?* Not only is it possible, but it has become increasingly obvious that today's companies will achieve their greatest success not despite their leaders' most deeply held values—but because of them. This is the essence of *Trust, Inc.*: the power of a management structure that adopts the practice of the alignment of values through all levels of corporate life. Alignment is an ethical shorthand that allows all individuals in the organization to move ahead as quickly and efficiently as possible under all circumstances. Rather than view trust as a matter of simply following rules—the "old accountability"—we called upon leaders to consider what it really takes to tackle the complexities of a values-based organization, as well as to anticipate the positive results. It is also vital to pay heed to the values operating, often invisibly, beneath the surface of everyday decisions and throughout organizational life.

Knowing our own and other people's values is an important place to begin. However, as we now know, cultivating trust takes more than simply feeling or thinking that we know what the right thing is for us or others to do in any given situation. In fact, dedication to honesty, consistency and courage often demands that we recognize when we are somewhere in the gray. For instance, in regards to our values and beliefs, especially in the global marketplace, we may be equal, but especially when it comes to complex ethical issues, it can be a mistake to assume that we are "all the same." While taking comfort in the realization that our similarities are greater than our differences, it is critical for leaders to address the core questions of how and why it is that even good people don't always agree, and how we can nevertheless go about building trust with one another, especially when it really matters. In our experience, trust is advanced or damaged in an organization, one issue, decision, act or interaction at a time. It is the primary task of the ethical leader to establish credibility by seeking the underlying patterns operating beneath the surface of challenges, identifying root causes. If you solve only the symptom, the problem at hand will re-emerge—perhaps in different and even more toxic forms—somewhere down the line.

In the end, we argue that business has to be personal and that it is the leader's responsibility to flow his or her ethics through the company, setting the standard to which all levels of organizational life will aspire. Research shows that the more resilient people are, the more they can be counted on to do the right thing, even under adverse, pressured circumstances. While it is true that some people are born resilient, for most people, resilience is a quality that requires periodic lifelong development. The leader who can be counted upon to build rather than breach trust has taken the time to identify his or her ultimate values: those things that are meaningful and attainable regardless of one's external circumstances. The importance of the practice of alignment between individual values and corporate goals cannot be emphasized enough. Those leaders who take a proactive role in implementing organizational strategies that support the advancement of a values-based corporate culture are most likely to reap the rewards of building trust on every level—and under any circumstance. Employee morale is raised, the bottom line is enhanced and all organizational energies can be invested in building for the future.

So, how does one "do" trust? *Trust, Inc.* concludes that ethical leaders are those inspirational, self-aware individuals who prove themselves to be unabashed in the face of uncertainty. They do not fear that obstacles will get in the way of their goals—they trust that they will. Their great gift is knowing that whatever challenges do arise, their spirits will be greater. This is the stuff of heroes: be it launching a global marketing campaign, or taking a lonely ethical stance because it is, above all, the right thing to do.

When it comes to ethics, knowing your values can sometimes feel like a terrible nuisance…but it's also the key to self-respect as well as organizational vitality. Bridging the gap between personal values and organizational goals unleashes the power of alignment for unprecedented organizational productivity, heightened employee morale and personal satisfaction when doing the right thing. This is no small feat. Leaders who win the trust of their various constituencies understand that paying heed to their convictions may require something more of them than they wish they'd have to give. Nevertheless, ethical leaders discover over and over again that their greatest influence, power and success will come as a side product of their willingness to do the right thing, time after time.

We salute you, our readers, who are undertaking the serious task of learning to "do" trust. Flow your values down through your organizations and out to your stakeholders and you will have a foundation of mutual trust upon which truly great enterprises can be built.

1) Understand Right from wrong
2) Do right thing each time a
   Choice comes.

Looking Forward

It was nearly one year ago, over a steaming pot of tea, that we discovered our shared sense of urgency about the role of trust in regards to organizational leadership. Since then, our passion for the subject has grown exponentially as issues related to ethics and accountability have jumped off the business pages and into front-page headlines.

With every passing day, it is increasingly apparent that in regards to the alignment of values and goals, the institutions of not only business, but government, education and even the family need to be repaired. Too many organizational leaders continue to be driven by greed and self-interest. It is not only the CEO in the corner suite who is culpable, nor do all the ramifications of breaches of trust play out as headline news.

Contributing to our damaged institutions are investors who overpaid for a deal and then placed unrealistic pressures on management to perform. Also playing a role are employees who have given up trying, dragging themselves to their jobs, working at a level below their potential and returning home feeling unfulfilled. Even in our families, too many of us give up on the hard work of cultivating mutual values too quickly—when we even try at all. Depleted, home lives suffer as the statistics regarding divorce send an alarming signal. Educators also set the bar too low, allowing their institutions to give a pass to mediocrity, while failing to inspire their students to think about what matters most.

Rectification must begin at the top, and we are hopeful as we also encounter an increasing number of organizational leaders who are taking the time to define their values, making the effort to weave those values into every decision, act and encounter. Not only are their stated commitment to values generating power and intensity, but even more encouraging is the trend toward leadership behavior that is consistent with those values.

We know there are issues but we also know they can be fixed. May our generation of leaders become known for having taken up the task of setting the highest standards for values and ethics at all levels of organizational and personal life. Looking forward, we know that you will prove our theory right: your greatest success will come not despite your most deeply held values—but because of them.

Thank you for joining us in taking up the serious task of learning to "do" trust.

Judith Rogala
Carol Orsborn

For more information, visit our website.
www.trustincthebook.com

Beebe, John. *Integrity in Depth.* New York, NY.: Fromm International, 1995.

Boatright, John R. *Ethics and the Conduct of Business,* 4th Ed., Upper Saddle River, NJ.: Prentice Hall, 2003.

Brown, Marvin T. *The Ethical Process: An Approach to Disagreements and Controversial Issues,* 3rd Ed. Upper Saddle River, NJ.: Prentice Hall, 2003.

Campbell, Joseph and Moyers, Bill. *The Power of Myth.* New York, NY.: Doubleday, 1988.

Collins, Jim. *Good to Great.* New York, NY.: Harper Business, 2001.

De Bono, Edward. *De Bono's Course in Thinking.* New York, NY.: Facts on File, Inc., 1994.

Fukuyama, Francis. *Trust: The Social Virtues and the Creation of Prosperity.* London, UK.: Penguin Books, 1996.

Garfield, Charles et al. *The Soul of Business.* Carlsbad, CA.: Hay House, Inc., 1997.

Hartman, Laura P. *Perspectives in Business Ethics,* 2nd Ed. Boston, Mass.: McGraw-Hill Irwin, 2002.

Hinman, Lawrence M. *Ethics: A Pluralistic Approach to Moral Theory.* New York, NY: Harcourt Brace College Publishers, 1998.

Johnson, Craig E. *Meeting the Ethical Challenges of Leadership.* Thousand Oaks, CA.: Sage Publications, 2001.

Lawrence, Anne G., Weber, James and Post, James E. *Business in Society.* New York, NY.: McGraw-Hill/Irwin, 2005.

Lewis, Hunter. *A Question of Values.* Mt. Jackson, VA. Axios Press, 2000.

McLemore, Clinton W. *Street-Smart Ethics*. Louisville, KY.: Westminster John Knox Press, 2003.

Mitroff, Ian I. and Denton, Elizabeth A. *A Spiritual Audit of Corporate America*. San Francisco, CA.: Jossey-Bass Publishers, 1999.

Orsborn, Carol. *The Art of Resilience*. New York, NY.: Three Rivers Press, 1997.

Orsborn, Carol. *How Would Confucius Ask for a Raise*. New York, NY.: Avon Books, 1998.

Orsborn, Carol. *Inner Excellence at Work*. New York, NY.: Amacom Books, 1999.

Orsborn, Carol. *Solved by Sunset*. New York, NY.: Crown Publishing, 1995.

"Restoring Trust in Business: Models for Action," New York, NY.: The Public Relations Coalition, 2004.

Singer, Peter, ed. *A Companion to Ethics*. Oxford, UK.: Blackwell Publishers, 2002.

Trevino, Linda Klebe and Weaver, Gary R. *Managing Ethics in Business Organizations*. Stanford, CA.: Stanford Business Books, 2003.

ACKNOWLEDGEMENTS

The values that are the basis for this book came from my loving parents, who taught me to trust and believe in myself and others. Their lives ended too early, but they left behind a legacy of courage, respect and integrity. I attribute my firm belief in myself—and the success that it has brought to my life—to my parents; my brother, Tom; and my sister, Susan. They have always been there to support me. How wonderful to see the legacy passed on to my two nephews, Christopher and John, who clearly understand the values of life.

I have been fortunate to work with so many dedicated people like Joan Beugen, Carolyn Dugan, Janet Diederichs and Alan Gohlke who never shirked from their commitments or from doing the "right thing" even in the face of adversity.

Special thanks to Fred Smith of FedEx. He is a great leader and his belief in taking care of your people was a critical success factor for FedEx.

This book is a dream come true and a cadre of people helped to make it happen, primarily, Carol Orsborn. My thanks to Dr. Tessa Warschaw for introducing us. Because they believed and lived the dream with me, I gratefully acknowledge the contributions of: Marilyn Bishop, Dee Campbell, The Cimarron Leadership Team, Bradley Costello, Rick Hampton, Jane Kroner, Jeff Larkin, Nancy Markwell, Tom McGarry, Lisa Miskimins, Ken Norgan, Judy Rosener, Ph.D., Carol Schlichting, and Dennis Spina—thank you for enriching the lives of so many, including mine.

And finally, both Carol and I thank Suzie Isaacs and her designer, David Robson, for exceptional guidance through the publishing process. We couldn't have published this book without them.

Judith A. Rogala

I am proud that the last book my mother listened to me spin was this one—a book about her favorite topic, values. I will be grateful forever to my Mom and Dad for supporting my writing career and for inspiring me through the quality of their own deeds and aspirations.

I gratefully acknowledge the contributions of my students in the doctoral program in organizational leadership at Pepperdine University. Also, my Deans—Bob Paull and Farzin Madjujik—for inviting me to teach there. I also want to thank my clients, especially Steve Milovich at the Walt Disney Company, for encouraging me to reach out to corporations. You were right. There is both a need and a demand for ethics and resilience training.

A special thank you to my co-author and fellow mountain climber, Judith Rogala. You are an inspiration.

Finally, I want to thank my husband, Dan, and my children, Grant and Jody—the best fellow travelers one could wish for in life.

Carol Orsborn, Ph.D.

Judith Rogala began her career with Trans World Airlines, rising rapidly from flight attendant to senior management. Known for her ability to assess issues quickly and implement productive solutions, Rogala was recruited by Federal Express early in the company's history. She was Vice President for sales and services throughout Canada and 17 central states, contributing to FedEx's growth from a $300 million company to over $7 billion in her decade-long tenure. Promoted to Senior Executive, Rogala managed 20,000 employees throughout the world in such disciplines as hub operations, properties and facilities, engineering and logistics.

After assuming a leadership role on the team that merged Flying Tigers Cargo into FedEx, she was recruited to serve as President and CEO of Flagship Express, a worldwide NASDAQ cargo airline company. Over the past several decades, Rogala has served in senior leadership positions in a wide range of companies, specializing in turn-arounds and startups. Among her credits is the establishment of the Business Services Division for Office Depot and leadership of ARAMARK Uniform Services, serving more than 400,000 businesses.

Rogala has an established consulting practice which is focused on ethical business leadership. A lifelong athlete as well as business leader, she also has had a long term association with The Catapult Factor, a California-based leadership training organization that uses mountain climbing as the life changing means to expand individual, professional and team boundaries. She also lectures to students in the Graduate School of Management at the University of California-Irvine. Rogala received her Master's Degree in Business Administration from the University of New Mexico, and has served on a number of civic, community and corporate boards including Butler Manufacturing, Red Roof Inns and DSC Logistics.

Carol Orsborn, Ph.D. is the author of ten highly regarded books—translated into 13 languages—on various aspects and applications of values in work and life, including *The Art of Resilience* (Three Rivers Press). She is President of Orsborn Communications, an award-winning firm providing values-based communications and consultation to clients such as The Walt Disney Company, Burson-Marsteller Worldwide and PacifiCare. She is professor of ethics and society (adj.) at Pepperdine University and a research associate at the University of California Los Angeles (UCLA) Center for the Study of Religion. Her doctorate from Vanderbilt University is in the history and critical theory of religion, with emphasis on values formation. She has presented papers at a number of academic conferences, most recently on ethical decision-making at the Society for Business Ethics, where she serves as Communications Managing Director.